How to Forgive and Move On

Jenny Hare

Jenny Hare is a trained counsellor and relationship therapist. She was *Woman's Weekly*'s agony aunt and advice columnist for more than 17 years. As a general counsellor, she specializes in helping others live positively and happily. She delights in living in the country, painting and writing with great joy. She is the author of 11 books.

Teach® Yourself

How to Forgive and Move On

Jenny Hare

Acknowledgements

With thanks to my wonderful sister Penny Stanway and to
Angela Lloyd-Jones, Christine Thomas, Philip Shanks and
Laura Vettori for their wisdom and thoughtful comments. Also
to Victoria Roddam and Robert Anderson, my editors, for their
inspiration, help and support.

Contents

Introduction

Forgive. The very word has a warm, welcoming feel because it's all about giving. And when we forgive, or live forgivingly in all sorts of ways, we give something to ourselves as well as others. Forgiveness is a blessing that has the potential to heal, to restore and to soothe. It can change the dynamic of conflict and hate to resolution and a workable peace.

Forgiveness may be spontaneous, in the moment, or a step-by-step process. It can be complex, yet is sometimes simple. It isn't limited to a single act, and it isn't hard work, goody-goody or a fantasy. Forgiveness, like love, can be at the heart of our lives, and, when it is, it transforms our lives, lifting our spirits in so many ways.

One of the great things about forgiveness is that it's our choice. Even in circumstances where it's impossible to forgive someone, we can, in living forgivingly, not just survive the trauma or hurt but move on, free of negative emotions such as blame and resentment.

It's a tremendous relief to forgive or live forgivingly, for in doing so you let go of negativity. Freed from the pain of bitterness, you can recover and in time enjoy life to the full again.

So every time you blame and judge, think of the alternative of forgiving. If you recoil at the difficulty of the prospect, start out by becoming a detective. Attitudes and habits are caused by the events and influences we have experienced. Just as prejudice is learned and becomes a habit when fostered, so is an unforgiving stance. Hurt happens to all of us. You've been hurt and my heart goes out to you. Every single hurt is sore, even the smaller ones we feel almost every day. But by gaining an understanding of yourself and your background, you can learn to deal with these blows so they perhaps don't wound you at all and certainly don't wreck your life.

Understanding forgiveness and your ability to be forgiving is an adventure – it's absorbing, fascinating, and life- and happiness-affirming. It's part of your own story and the key to transforming the way you react to life's arrows and sorrows.

Forgiveness is a revelation. And every time we forgive or even remember how it feels to forgive, it feels heart-warming all over again. And that's what forgiveness is about. We do it again, and again and again. Several times a day perhaps – countless times throughout our lives. It always transforms how we feel and often, though we may not see it, in some way it also transforms the other person, our relationship with them and/or the situation.

You probably know some people who have an aura of warmth and calm, and you probably noticed how people behave better in their presence. They're less carping, they make fewer swipes at others' expense – perhaps they refrain from these behaviours altogether. You can be one of these people: naturally assuming the goodness in all of us, naturally forgiving the not so good side we all have. You can make a difference just like this. You can be one of the world's peacemakers.

For the ability and willingness to forgive are catching. Just as, for instance, you encourage other people to be positive when you are positive yourself, or to follow your example in being warm and friendly, so will people notice when you say or do something in the spirit of forgiveness and reconciliation. It may stop them in their well-worn tracks of quick readiness to criticize and judge. It may make them think how much better it is to encourage peace and realize how good it feels when they do.

Forgiving and living forgivingly are always an option, and all it takes to start being forgiving is to stop saying you can't or won't or will never forgive and allow yourself the possibility of forgiving instead.

The possibility is the beginning of freedom from hurt and the start of a wonderful journey along the path of forgiveness.

The Teach Yourself Breakthrough series has a number of features to help you get the most out of reading this book. *How to Forgive and Move On* includes the following boxed features:

 'Key idea' boxes that distil the most important ideas and thoughts

 'Remember this' boxes to help you take away what really matters

 'Try it now' boxes to provide you with useful exercises and techniques

 'Focus points' at the end of each chapter to help you hone in on the core message of each chapter.

At the end of the book you will also find a list of resources providing further information and help.

The meaning of forgiveness

In this chapter you will learn:

▶ *About the historical meanings of forgiveness*
▶ *How forgiveness can liberate us from negativity*
▶ *How it can be better to forgive silently rather than in words.*

Forgiveness is a healing balm. It comes in many forms. Forgiveness may be love in action, for example, or a well-thought-through rationalization of a situation. It may be using your ability to move forward without bitterness. Forgiving is a realm of possibility and makes sense in so many ways and on so many levels.

It feels good to live forgivingly – not only to forgive in specific instances when we're personally hurt, but above all as a way of living and behaving. How we forgive is very individual, but any one of us can make living forgivingly a habit. In individual situations the forgiving way forward depends on the various elements and what feels right – and possible – for you. Finding your kind of forgiveness can be like working out the clues in a detective story, and in this book we'll explore its wide-ranging scope.

Key idea

However we forgive or are forgiven, forgiveness is a blessing. It can be the smallest relief from the searing pain of anger or the wondrous joy of freedom from blame and hate – or something in between – but it always makes a life-enhancing difference.

The roots of forgiveness

We hear a lot about forgiveness today in terms of personal and social development and in regard to universal peace, but it has been an important feature of cultures around the globe across the ages. I like the feeling this sense of history gives us – it's as though all that forgiveness is always out there to cheer us on, comfort and strengthen us.

The accumulated wisdom of the past also helps our understanding now across the breadth and depth, and yes, the complexity, of forgiveness – what it means both to forgive and to accept forgiveness. It expands, subtly but very definitely, our ability to continue the practice and art of forgiving, both as a moral principle of inestimable value and an astonishingly therapeutic healing process in our present lives. Let's take a look at the history of forgiveness so that we can gain a sense of the ongoing blessing of forgiveness that we can revisit any time we need encouragement and inspiration.

WHERE THE WORD COMES FROM
The verb 'to pardon' comes from the Latin *perdonare*, which means 'to give completely and without reservation'. In the Germanic beginnings of English the syllables were translated as *for* (thoroughly) and *giefan* (to give). This word *forgiefan* meant in Old English 'to give up, allow'.

There's a lovely word corresponding to 'forgive' in Aramaic/ Syriac – *shbag* – which literally means 'to untie'. Although this is not a root for our word 'forgive', it can be useful in some situations to think of forgiving as being a way of untying or loosening the knots of resentment and judgement we create when we've been hurt or wronged.

The various definitions of the verb 'to forgive' and its meaning for us today include 'to pardon somebody for an offence', 'to renounce anger' and 'to abandon a claim' … to excuse, to absolve, to exonerate. The most apt one for most of us is renouncing anger. Every time we do that it's a relief – a release from tension and pain.

Key idea
Forgiving in any of its forms frees us to enjoy our health and happiness.

Remember this
All of the meanings of forgiveness help us to remember that forgiving isn't necessarily something we do for and about another person. It's more about *the way we are*. Forgiving is about giving, and when we are compassionate, kind, generous, loving, thoughtful, honest, sensitive or fair – to others and ourselves – we are living in a forgiving way.

PHILOSOPHICAL REFERENCES, CLASSIC AND CONTEMPORARY
Over the centuries philosophers have been fascinated with the concept of forgiveness. They've discussed whether forgiving is

an act of will or possible only when the hurt or offended person has the necessary character trait to be forgiving, or whether both are necessary. It's suggested that it involves resisting the spontaneous or learned reaction of resentment towards the perpetrator of the hurt and refusing to blame them. Forgiveness, it has been argued, doesn't attempt to justify, condone or minimize the wrong done. Someone who forgives is regarded as having a compassionate nature and being generally a kind person. This kindness, this readiness not to blame and this ability to find compassion in your heart for the wrongdoer, while not necessarily empathizing with them, resonates with several religions, as we will see in Chapter 8: Forgiveness and religion.

The concept of forgiving stretches our minds as we try to make sense of the different nuances and the difficulties, or even apparent impossibility, of forgiving where cruelty has been involved and/or where there is a lack of remorse.

Remember this

If you are ready to be still and listen out for it, the very thought of forgiveness transcends bitterness, hurt and resentment, giving a respite from them and creating an opening for peace and the notion that, as Julian of Norwich put it, 'All is well, all will be well.'

That's not to deny that resentment and outrage are natural, understandable and, indeed, proper reactions. Sometimes healthy self-respect and respect of cultural moral boundaries demand that we stand up for ourselves, refusing where possible to be abused again or otherwise victimized. We must be prepared, too, to fight for justice.

Key idea

Forgiveness doesn't mean we should let evil flourish but that we should not perpetuate another kind of evil by indulging in pernicious ongoing blame, shame and reciprocal hate. Rather, forgiveness cleans the slate, allowing healing and creating a habitat where healthy mutual respect can germinate and grow.

SOME THOUGHTS ON FORGIVENESS

Forgiveness, like charity, often begins at home. Many thinkers have noted that we are most likely to hurt the people we love and the following case study highlights the importance of being ready to forgive each other easily.

Case study: How 'DP' learned to say sorry

'DP' consulted me because she and her husband were having rows that spoiled their everyday relationship and were threatening their prospect of long-term togetherness. I asked her to remember how her family had approached forgiveness when she was a child and her face lit up as she began to speak:

'Familiarity, my mother used to say, can all too easily breed contempt. She and my dad never went to bed with a dispute unsettled. They always said sorry to each other and told each other "I love you." They taught me and my brother to do the same.'

I asked her to share this with her husband and try it out. I explained that to let crossness with each other fester overnight often 'sets' it for several days, whereas somehow the very act of saying 'Sorry' or 'Let's agree to differ' and giving each other a hug allows the conflict to evaporate.

Next time we met she said: 'He agreed and we soon tried it out, as we had an argument the very next evening. We duly said "Sorry" to each other before we went to sleep and it was quite funny – we had to laugh as it was so different from the usual fuming! It seemed to draw us together. Next morning we decided what to do about the problem – actually, it was easy to compromise as in the light of day we both felt constructive, and because the mutual 'sorry' had taken away the anger, we worked together. It really works and we're going to make saying sorry our habit from now on.'

Over and over again it's been noted that we can learn to forgive and, like this couple, shed our anger at each other. We can do it on our own but counselling can be helpful, too, and I've often seen how powerful and supportive group therapy can also be in bringing about an understanding of the viability and benefits of forgiveness along with a willingness to give it a go.

Throughout the history of literature, novelists have written stories depicting the misery of ongoing, engrained resentment, bitterness and hate and the blessed relief when these are given up. And when the label of 'victim', whether imposed by others or ourselves, is renounced, the sense of freedom, peace and inner strength can be astonishingly good.

Mahatma Gandhi, one of the world's greatest forgivers, said that forgiveness is an attribute of the strong. He meant, I think, that forgiving is an act of will that takes both an initial decision to forgive, backed up by reason, and an ongoing determination and perseverance to keep going with it. It's by no means a soft option. It takes guts, strength and stamina. But living forgivingly feels good in this sense: it's far easier than not forgiving, which feels terrible and can be soul-destroying.

Others have pointed out that when we forgive we improve our psychological and physical health and restore our sense of personal power. Specific forgiveness may lead to reconciliation between the offended and offender or help groups in conflict to resolve difficulties and make peace.

Try it now: Make a pact

Make a pact with your nearest and dearest (partner, child, friend – anyone you live with or are close to) that, next time you fall out, you'll make it up with each other before the end of the day. It just means saying to each other: 'I'm sorry.'

('I love you' is a great addition.)

How we 'grow' forgiveness

Key idea

As we progress through our lives, the ability to forgive is learned and then ebbs and flows, growing as we mature and often bringing a late flowering of peace and goodwill as acceptance and forgiveness become our way of being.

We're born neither forgiving nor unforgiving but are generally pretty accepting of others, expecting the best. We learn from our parents not to be quick to blame and retaliate, be vindictive or hold a grudge. We learn from experience that most things that seem outrageous to us in the moment are soon forgotten and all is well again. We find that, on the whole, we get what we give out – when we share with our friends and enjoy their company, the chances are they'll get on well with us, too.

Come our late teens and twenties, we can't believe the way adults run the world for all the talk of tolerance. We observe their sparring and warring, hating and blaming and we want peace, with all our conviction and passion. How can our elders make such a terrifying, desperate mess of things? Disappointed, we become resigned to our inability to live in harmony within our families, let alone with other communities nationally and globally. Sadly, we may join the moaners and groaners of the world, blaming others harshly, storing up bitterness, finding it difficult, or perhaps refusing, to forgive.

Try it now: Change your perspective for a moment

1 Next time someone is acting impossibly badly and you're being judgemental, put yourself in their shoes. Imagine you are them. How does it feel? What are you thinking? Why are you behaving like this? Why are you so upset?
2 Now be yourself again. Notice how your attitude to them has altered with the understanding you've gained. Feel the compassion for their anxiety/pain.
Remember, it doesn't mean you're condoning their behaviour; you are simply understanding it in some way a bit better. This is a form of the forgiving path.

As we mature, hopefully learning a bit more about life and love and realizing the sheer frailty of humanity, we come to realize that, because of our individual circumstances, we behave differently from others and not always well. We take heed of the maxim 'There but for fortune go you or I' and realize the truth that we cannot know another person's heart unless we walk in their shoes. Compassion comes back to us. We discover again how good it is to forgive ourselves and others.

Willingness to forgive is often a sign both of the innocence and innate wisdom of youth and the learned wisdom of a lifetime's experience and thought. However, we can adopt and practise forgiveness at any age in between.

Forgiveness is a yardstick of emotional and spiritual maturity, and – whatever your age – it lights up your life.

What does it mean to forgive – does it mean forgetting?

There are many kinds of forgiveness and many degrees to which we forgive.

Any true attempt to forgive – even just the wish to – is better than none and will lift your spirits.

Remember this
Forgiving isn't about claiming the moral high ground and/or a kind of martyrdom; it's a simple letting go of further blaming and shaming, rancour and bitterness.

You might not be able to forgive someone completely or even at all. We forgive according to our present ability and the nature of the hurt, but we can always choose to let go of its grip. Again and again, we see people forgive those who have inflicted the worst kinds of cruelty, loss and other hurt on them. Sometimes it's unreserved forgiveness, sometimes it's a letting go (remember *shbag*!) – an untying of the noose from around our brain and heart.

Forgiveness isn't dependent on forgetting – it's valid and valuable in its own right.

However we are able to forgive, it's not always a one-act wonder. Traumatic memories will resurface unasked along with, perhaps, the old feelings of outrage, fear and anger. Then we forgive again. And again, and again and again, and doing so is a blessing, a relief, a freeing up.

Try it now: Wash yourself clean of anger

Next time a bad memory of someone hurting you comes up and rage unexpectedly overwhelms you again, forgive them again. If you can, say in your mind the words 'I forgive them' and let the anger flow away. Or, if you can't forgive them, in your mind let a feeling of love and compassion for yourself flood over you, washing away the anger.

Beware of being patronizing!

Oscar Wilde said that the best way to annoy someone is to forgive them for something: 'Always forgive your enemies – nothing annoys them so much.' This always makes me laugh – but there's a lot to learn from it, too! When someone tells you unasked that they're prepared to forgive you, it implies they've judged you and that you've done something wrong and they are the innocent party. True or not, the unbidden forgiveness is likely to infuriate you.

Similarly, it's best not to claim to forgive someone for actions inflicted on someone else. One friend, who readily regretted the way she'd behaved in a certain situation, was gobsmacked when an acquaintance who had nothing to do with it said to her: 'I forgive you.' 'Who does she think she is – God?' exclaimed my exasperated friend.

So do beware of being pompous and patronizing in the way you forgive. Almost always, it's better to say nothing and to forgive silently and inwardly. Remember that it's not only, if at all, a gift for the one who's hurt you – it's for yourself. Unless someone expressly asks you to forgive them, forgiveness is best left unspoken.

However, there are times when we are beset with guilt for a hurt we've caused someone that we long to be forgiven. And when that forgiveness comes, all we need do is to accept it as wholeheartedly as it is offered, and feel the generosity of compassion and goodwill that prompted it.

How forgiveness frees us from a range of negative emotions

The negative emotions hurt causes are complex. Often, we're taken first by surprise as most of us are naturally trusting that others will be pleasant to us. From there our emotions can range across shock, outrage, fear, defensiveness, anger, rage and disbelief and leave a lasting legacy of bitterness, resentment, blame and a desire for revenge. All feel horrible and, in disrupting our personal peace and sleep, spoil our life in countless ways.

Any kind of forgiving attitude lessens this burden of negativity – the more holistically we forgive, the more psychological freedom we gain. And when we are free of blame and shame, we can behave and live positively. It feels good.

As negativity moves out, positivity moves in. The more forgiving we are, the more positive we are, enabling us to reclaim our peace, our joy, our life.

Key idea

Simply contemplating the possibility of forgiveness is a catalyst that instantly lifts some of the negativity of blame and anger. As negative emotions lessen in any way, your whole system relaxes. It's all to do with your body's natural balancing and healing ability – homeostasis – but you will find out more about that, as well as about all the aspects of forgiveness introduced in this chapter, throughout this book.

Focus points

✳ Forgiveness is a way of giving to ourselves and others. It frees us from blame and bitterness and blesses us with love.
✳ Forgiveness takes many forms, including being compassionate and fair.
✳ Being forgiving is a choice you can make and it feels good.
✳ Readiness to make and/or accept an apology helps you heal.
✳ Being willing to forgive ourselves and others is a great strength and a sign of wisdom.

Next step

In Chapter 2, First steps to forgiving, we'll look at some of the ways in which we can choose to forgive and accept forgiveness, not just as occasional acts but by taking on the whole spectrum of forgiveness as a way of life.

First steps to forgiving

In this chapter you will learn:

▶ *How to nurture a forgiving way of being*

▶ *That sometimes when we find offence it is our own behaviour that has led to it*

▶ *How thinking 'you, me and we' instead of 'I, I, I' can be more fulfilling*

▶ *How self-understanding can create the conditions for forgiveness.*

Forgiveness starts now. It's in the moments of this day and every day. Every moment is a different starting point – the rest of your life begins here – isn't that an amazing, inspirational thought? We're so used to walking along with one foot in the past, it's mind-boggling to register that actually you don't have to. The past is the past. By all means remember with happiness the good of the past and carry it with you to warm you along the way, but don't linger in the bad and definitely don't hang on to it.

Key idea

The present starts now – the future is yours to step into, unfettered by resentment and bitterness, unkind thoughts and unresolved regrets.

There are so many ways to forgive and follow a forgiving way of life; here are some helpful first steps to find your own way and get going.

Deciding on your aim

Focusing on your intention to live forgivingly – that is, well, kindly and fairly – is a great beginning. When we project an idea, we move along with it and towards it subconsciously as well as consciously. It makes it so much easier to fulfil, and it's surprisingly fulfilling along the way. It's such an exciting, feel-good course of action that you may think you want to do it all – the whole spectrum of forgiveness – right away.

Remember this

Being forgiving is complex and often multi-layered, so there's much to learn about yourself and others, and much to practise. It's interesting and often surprising, so take time to enjoy the quest step by step.

Remembering that a forgiving attitude is your choice, now and every day

If you're feeling decidedly unforgiving, don't worry. You're bound to have spontaneous thoughts that aren't forgiving.

It's so easy to criticize and blame others, and to sabotage your own self-esteem, too. The forgiving path isn't about ignoring negative feelings – they may be very valid and it's important to notice and review them. But you don't have to get them out of all proportion and/or obsess about them – that won't do anyone any good, least of all yourself. Constructively and positively working out the best way forward is the key. That automatically guides you to take an overview of the situation, allowing you to see all the various viewpoints and aspects clearly. Your understanding will then become wider and deeper and you'll feel a lot better and be in a much better frame of mind to act fairly.

NOTICING THOUGHTS

Forgiveness is there alongside the thoughts that come into your mind – the invited ones when you're thinking through something as well as the spontaneous ideas. Openness is part of it – being honest about and with yourself. Self-understanding follows and helps you to be less judgemental and more forgiving in other ways, too.

Remember this

You are in control of your thoughts. You can *choose* to think forgivingly.

Keeping calm

If you're hurt or angry, you'll probably feel fraught and the more stressed out you get the harder it is to be tolerant, let alone empathic. Although it can be infuriating when someone else tells you to calm down, telling yourself to do so is astonishingly effective and it's possible to stop anxiety in its tracks by simply deciding to stay calm and chill out. Just remember that it's *your* mind and *you* are at the controls of it.

A wry sense of humour helps tremendously. Are there any catchphrases that make you smile? They can be useful as instant smile-makers and relaxers. A friend of mine swears by the one from the much beloved UK television series *Dad's Army*: 'Don't panic, Captain Mainwaring!' My friend says: 'It makes me giggle inside and giggling is a great stress buster.' Oddball's devastatingly laid-back line from *Kelly's Heroes* has the same effect for me: 'Don't make with the negative vibes, man.' And then there's the immortal ending of the film *Monty Python's Life of Brian* when Brian sings 'Always look on the bright side of life...'

This may sound flippant, but I learned from my mother and her friends who, like her, were nurses in war zones that in times of stress there's nothing like humour for helping you hold on and cope. A sense of humour, bizarre as it may seem, can help us keep it together in dire circumstances and stay within the forgiving spectrum.

Stopping a fracas or feud before it begins

Catchphrases are also great for flashing a warning sign whenever we're in danger of developing a grudge against someone.

Case study: How Dan rediscovered an old catchphrase

I asked a counsellee, Dan, to think of a catchphrase that would help him control his tendency to take against people easily. He remembered: 'Even as little kids, my sister and I were aware that Mum, usually so kind and caring, was ultra-sensitive. If someone said or did something unkind to her, her first reaction was to get into a strop about it and sound off, not to the person, but to us. Dad knew it, too, and would say to her quietly: "Don't get up against them." It was a good catalyst; the familiarity of it was all it took for her to let go of her indignation and relax.'

Dan realized that he was as sensitive as his mother and decided to try using his father's mantra: 'Don't get up against them.' Next time we met he said it had already proved helpful in helping him let it go when someone said something that seemed offensive.

Another popular British English phrase is 'Don't get your knickers in a twist.' It's funny and speaks volumes about how annoying being irritated can be – and somehow saying it is all that it takes to calm you down and not 'get up against' someone.

A former neighbour of mine would frequently sound off about a difference of opinion with someone, and all it took to soothe his ruffled feathers was for another neighbour to say wryly: 'Good job we're not all the same, isn't it, Barry?'

Key phrases like these are great reminders that life's too short to take against someone, allowing us to pre-empt rising conflict and slip back gracefully into harmony and, where necessary, resolve disputes constructively.

Remember this

Ultra-sensitive touchiness is self-centred and never helps. The forgiving way is the way of peace and, where that's not possible, rational, unemotional thought will show you the best way forward.

Remember who you are

Remember and keep remembering that you are essentially kind and well meaning. I'm assuming this because you're reading this book and because the vast majority of us are good-hearted. As the veteran British journalist Kate Adie writes in her book *The Kindness of Strangers*, even in war-torn countries people are still kind in the midst of the conflict and horror. Everyday life is full of kindness, too – it's our default setting.

Yet there's a strange paradox in the newspapers regarding kindness today. While acts of kindness and courage are celebrated and those who display them are much praised for their goodness, we also often find columnists picking on people in a spitefully critical way on a very personal level. So, on the one hand, we're encouraged to be kind ourselves, but, on the other, there are examples of unnecessary nastiness dressed up as entertainment. It's the same on real-life television shows where the contestants are encouraged to be vile to each other – it makes, say the producers, 'great television'. It creates such a lot of hurt and bad feeling that forgiveness is needed more than ever.

It isn't clever to be nasty and it certainly doesn't *feel* good.

So don't be spiteful. Instead, demonstrate and celebrate, every day, the kindness that is your essential being.

Remember you're human as well as humane

Just because you're humane, like to do your best and know others do, too, doesn't mean turning a blind eye to the not-so-good aspects of your personality and behaviour. Take the 'e' off humane and you're human – not perfect, not always caring of others, let alone nice about them. But part of forgiveness is being ready to recognize your inconsistencies and faults. Then you can try to improve, guarding against them and forgiving yourself when you let yourself down, just as you forgive others, to the best of your ability, when their behaviour's lacking. We're all on a learning curve in this life – stepping out onwards and upwards.

Balancing new thoughts and remembered ones

Key idea

The more you notice thoughts that call for a forgiving attitude, the more you'll remember how you're encouraging your forgiving nature and way of life, and the more it will develop. You'll notice more and more, too, how much forgiveness is needed.

Noticing yourself

This isn't about noticing others' wrongdoing or deficiencies. It's about noticing yourself – the way you are at the moment and how you're feeling. Do you feel warm and caring about others? Or maybe churlish and none too loving? How are you behaving and reacting to others' behaviour? Are you living up to your best?

However tough – skinned you like to think you are or show yourself to be, I expect you are, like most of us, sensitive to those around you. For, emotionally, practically, spiritually and socially, we resonate with everyone we meet on some level, however transitory our acquaintance. If you remember to be aware of this, in any encounter and every relationship you can choose to be forgiving. From compassion to full forgiveness there are many ways to feel for others and for yourself. It's all about remembering to be aware.

Taking out the ego

Ego is hugely powerful and, much of the time, pretty unpleasant. When we think 'I, I, I' it's all too often followed by verbs like 'want', 'hate', 'need' – by selfish, egotistical demands. It's the opposite of healthy self-esteem (whose close relationship with forgiveness we look at in Chapter 11). When ego takes us over, it tricks us into thinking not just that we 'deserve' something, as the ads would have us believe, but that we should have it as though it's somehow our right.

Remember this

A forgiving attitude and way of life remind us that we're all in this world together. Instead of 'me, me, me', forgiveness helps us think 'you, me and we'. We're all important, in our own way; we're all, at the same time, part of society, part of our world. Thinking forgivingly, we reach out to others and in interconnecting lines of communication and goodwill we can help each other get on together and find fulfilment.

Interestingly, when we are forgiving – be that acceptance, a loving reaching out to help, clemency or pardon – it often throws our supposed needs and wants into a clear perspective and we realize how unimportant and unessential they are and how much we already have.

In forgiving, we appreciate ourselves, others and the things that really matter.

Case study: How Mollie began to practise self-understanding

Mollie admitted to me that, while pretending to be understanding and pleasant to an acquaintance who could be awkward, in reality she was helping to stir conflict:

'A woman I don't like much at the club had a bit of a go at me. I decided to be magnanimous and, keeping calm, I debated the point she was making but was careful to keep smiling to show her and everyone how nice I am. She got crosser and crosser and in the end shouted at me and then flounced off.

'Later on, feeling decidedly unforgiving, and obsessing about how nasty she'd been, I made myself stand back and look rationally at what had happened.'

'Had you not been as nice as you'd tried to portray yourself, then?' I asked.

'No, I hadn't. In fact, I'd been rather sly – horrible word but forgiveness is all about being honest, isn't it? And I *was* sly. I'd smiled with my mouth, knowing full well that my heart wasn't smiling. I was actually icy cold to her. No wonder she got more frustrated and blew her top.'

'So had she not been wrong at all?' I prompted.

'It isn't about blame. That's what I want to get away from. The situation called for greater understanding and self- and mutual forgiveness. If we'd met and dealt with the problem on a level playing field, both of us authentically wanting to understand and deal with it fairly and pleasantly, we wouldn't have scrapped, would we? I've got a lot to practise – but at least I'm learning – and being more forgiving, as I go.'

'What has happened since?'

'She phoned me to say sorry for losing her rag. I said I'd been about to call her to apologize for being un-understanding and unhelpful. We're meeting tomorrow to work together on finding the best solution. No more aggression, active or passive. Together is the way forward.' She smiled and it was a smile of warmth, relief and enthusiasm.

...and you'll already be thinking of other wonderful things that are free to all of us and yet of inestimable value. Remember these things often and be glad.

Honestly acknowledging your part in what's happened

Once you've realized you've hurt someone, or they you, the next step is to resist slipping into defensive mode. We've all been there, busily claiming it wasn't our fault and coming up with endless excuses for our part in it. Sometimes, of course, we are totally blameless but, when we are partly responsible, recognizing it is an important prerequisite for forgiveness. In marriage, friendship and work relationships, every time we communicate we play a part and affect the way the interaction goes. Rather than defending your part, it's often illuminating to consider how you could have influenced the situation in a better way.

Facing the full implications and approaching the solution in a forgiving way

Recriminations, resentment, blame, shame – even the simplest of questions can be fraught with them. Three simple steps deal with them well – and often astonishingly effectively.

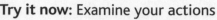

Try it now: Examine your actions

1 Like Mollie above, look insightfully into the way you felt, how you reacted and where you are now.

2 Consider other, better ways to deal with potential hurt and what's already flying around, and other negative feelings.

3 Join together, if possible, to look for the best way forward and, if that's not possible, do your own best to find a compromise or mutually satisfactory resolution.

Thawing out

One of the most unforgiving stances we can take is being frosty. Giving someone the 'ice treatment' is what psychologists call 'passive aggression' and it's very hurtful and confusing.

The following steps are a better way forward. They can restore harmony and a level ground for you both to address problems and seek constructive outcomes.

Try it now: Take steps to restore harmony

If you're tempted to go silent or cold towards someone who's upset you, be aware of it and think about it:

1 Acknowledge that the stance is the opposite of peacemaking.

2 Find it in your heart to feel compassion both for yourself and the other person.

3 Think of other ways to resolve the situation, keeping your dignity and firmly refusing to accept abuse of any kind, but if at all possible talking and behaving warmly and kindly.

Thinking before you speak

So often, being unkind is the last thing on our minds – and yet we open our mouths and say something hurtful. Being frank, outspoken or extrovert can be seen as admirable traits. But are they? Not if they give us licence to be unkind, harshly critical, insensitive and generally unforgiving. Spontaneity is a lovely concept – but, although it sounds like a contradiction, even the most spontaneous of us need to monitor what we're about to spout forth. It only takes a nanosecond to review it, asking 'Can this cause offence?' If it's 'yes', don't say it.

There's a great, useful saying worth remembering at all times: 'If you can't say something nice, don't say anything at all.' So often, we barge on in, consciously or unconsciously causing hurt to some degree. When it's conscious, it's wilful or, worse, cruel. When it's unconscious, it's careless or ignorant. We can all be conscious. I've been careless with words in the past and regretted it. I hope I won't be again, but it's something I need to be extra vigilant about, I know. The advice 'Engage your brain before speaking' may help you, as it does me, to button up whenever potentially hurtful words, thoughtless or not, threaten.

Focus points

* Cut out criticism and judgement and pause to think of a positive, constructive, kindly approach.
* Help someone in any way you can. It builds a bridge between you, transforming the atmosphere and situation.
* Take out the ego and replace it with a mixture of healthy self-esteem and humility. Instead of 'I, I, I', think 'You, me and we'.
* If someone behaves badly, check out whether you encouraged that in some way.
* Instead of seething or freezing with anger and blame, thaw out with understanding and a wish to seek a constructive way forward.

Next step

In Chapter 3, Health and forgiveness, we'll look at the beneficial impact on our health – body, mind and soul – of living forgivingly.

Health and forgiveness

In this chapter you will learn:

▶ *How taking a forgiving approach benefits our physical and psychological health*

▶ *How forgiving and moving on help reduce stress*

▶ *How adopting a compassionate attitude to others can help both them and us to heal.*

Is forgiveness an elixir of health? It certainly seems so, for every emotion we experience has a physical effect and it's long been known that, while negative feelings aren't good for our health, positive ones are a great tonic. Anger, for instance, raises our blood pressure while contentment lowers it.

What's being realized more and more is that every thought also has an impact on the brain and our emotions and therefore affects our physical and mental wellbeing. Scientists are investigating how this process works, but they are in agreement with doctors, psychologists and mental health workers that our personality and moods are tremendously important to our mental and physical health.

The physiological impact of living unforgivingly and shoring up emotions such as blame, shame, bitterness and martyrdom may damage other aspects of our physical health as well as making us feel pretty horrible.

Key idea

On the positive side of this equation, the wonderful realization is that forgiveness – whether it's actually letting go of or managing negative feelings towards someone or practising a kind, compassionate way of living generally – is healing mentally, emotionally, spiritually and physically.

It's not about pretending to forgive, though, or about trying to be an angel who never gets angry or experiences other negative emotions. We all have a plethora of genes, character traits and instincts we were born or imprinted with along the way that can lead us towards negative feelings, but fortunately we can monitor and control them.

Remember this

One of the secrets of the forgiving way of life is to notice your negative thoughts and impulses and let them go, as you let kindness and compassion flow into and through you instead.

When we live forgivingly like this, we're likely to:

▶ have lower blood pressure, heart rate and stress levels

▶ have fewer and/or less severe symptoms of any health conditions or illness we suffer from

▶ heal more quickly

▶ need less medication

▶ have more energy

▶ be more inspired to find and enjoy the pastimes we love and to enjoy life generally

▶ worry less and relax more

▶ get on with others

▶ experience less conflict and manage it without it getting us down

▶ explore, use and enjoy our creativity

▶ sleep soundly

▶ be happier and have the ability to be joyful

▶ live longer.

Try it now: Shrug away bitterness

1 Think of something you feel bitter about – it needn't be a huge grievance; something relatively unimportant will do fine.
2 Say aloud, if you're on your own (or in your mind, if not): 'I'm going to let go of this negativity and not think about it any more – or at least not until tomorrow when, if applicable, I will do something constructive about it.
3 Imagine that you are literally shrugging it off your shoulders.
4 Feel the relief of being free of the weight of it.

A counselee named Sarah, who was suffering from depression, agreed to try eliminating some of the grievances that were contributing to her unhappiness and anxiety. For example, she decided to waste no more time obsessing about her outrage against her local supermarket because she often had to queue for ages at the checkout.

'It sounds trivial,' she told me, 'but I keep grumbling about it.' Instead, she decided to write to the store manager, voicing her complaint and asking politely but firmly that in future he should arrange for more checkouts to be open at busy times. 'It's lovely getting rid of rumbling grievances like this,' she smiled. 'I was letting the store take over my thoughts, which was ridiculous and annoying in itself! I'm not going to obsess about things like that any more. I shall protest effectively whenever necessary, but from now on I refuse to let annoyances affect my wellbeing.'

The more she practised moving on from small grievances, the more she felt able to deal forgivingly with larger issues. Her depression began to lift as positivity was enabled to thrive.

The chemistry of forgiveness

When someone is compassionate towards us – even a stranger – we often feel there's a mysterious chemistry between us. It could be in an apparently small, everyday experience – for example, a caring dental worker who treats you like a real person rather than a set of teeth to be worked on, or a shop assistant who notices you're tired and speaks kindly to you.

Remember this

When someone is kind, you warm to them – you can't help it; it just happens. Your spirits are lifted, you feel physically better and stronger, too. You like them even though you hardly know them, and you feel they like you as well.

When someone behaves compassionately, their own brain is as beneficially affected by it as yours is by recognizing and receiving their kindness and interest. Both of you experience an uplift in wellbeing. That uplift again has a chemical effect on your brain, promoting mental and physical health.

It isn't a mystery. It really is about chemicals. One leading contender for chief catalytic hormone in this process is oxytocin. This chemical is sometimes thought of as the 'love chemical' because it's released when we're in love and when a mother bonds with her baby. It's also there in many pleasing social interactions. When it affects us we not only feel wonderful in the moment, but we're naturally more loving, caring and generally forgiving in our behaviour. It's also been discovered that oxytocin helps wounds heal more quickly.

Key idea

Your health and happiness will benefit – and thus your whole life – when you follow the forgiving way, not just in the small moments, influential though they are, but in your prime relationships.

Research has shown that kind people live longer. They certainly enjoy life more because compassion, kindness and the whole spectrum of the forgiving way feel good as well as benefitting your health.

The effects of forgiveness on stress

When we're frightened or feel threatened we automatically go into flight-or-fight mode. Both are brilliant when we are truly in peril, as the hormones adrenaline and cortisol triggered by stress and danger help us run fast or fight like demons. But the effect on our health – increased heart rate, soaring blood pressure and so on – is not so good if it happens repeatedly with everyday stresses and interpersonal worries such as conflict and imagined or real slights. Chronic or frequent stress may lead to several medical conditions including heart and gastro-intestinal problems, migraine and other kinds of headache, eating disorders and depression, as well as other mental illnesses.

The good news is that we can manage our response to the myriad potential causes of stress that we encounter in our lives. There are many simple but highly effective ways, for instance:

- Breathe slowly and deeply to balance the oxygen and carbon dioxide levels in your system. A useful guide is to breathe in to a count of 4, hold your breath as you count to 7 and exhale to a count of 8.

- Pause your busy-ness and take a break to meditate or find calmness. Even a couple of minutes' quiet, focusing on your breathing as above or following your favorite meditation technique, can dramatically reduce stress and return you to your forgiving way of life, but if you can do this for longer so much the better.

- Take some exercise. Swimming and walking are my own favourite uplifters and de-stressors and they don't put too much pressure on joints – but anything that you love and feel good doing is great.

- Daydream about a favourite pastime – or something you would love to do.

- Think of someone you care about – bask in the love you feel.

Try it now: Access your compassion

1 Sit quietly for a few minutes, breathing slowly and deeply.
2 Imagine you are walking along a beautiful beach with someone you are angry with. The tide is out and the sand is firm under your feet.
3 Imagine that they sincerely regret hurting you and that you accept their apology and suddenly feel a deep sense of compassion. You don't have to say 'I forgive you' unless you want to. The compassion you feel is for the sorrow that's been caused you, for their own pain and for others' suffering in the same kind of way.
4 Feel the sense of forgiveness in the beauty of the landscape and the air you are breathing.
5 Sense how the feeling of compassion is like a life-giving tonic and enables you to let go of your anger.
6 Even if you feel it's impossible to forgive someone, the feeling of compassion is always there for you to experience, and whenever you choose to access it, it will boost your strength and wellbeing.

The healing power of forgiveness

When you forgive someone you'll notice immediately the relief you feel. Gone is the tension of feeling judgemental, gone the nagging or acute pain of bitterness, gone the relentless resentment. In their place comes a feeling of freedom from all that negativity and a welcome return to positivity. All the health benefits of a forgiving way of life noted earlier apply to specific acts of forgiving. And there is a huge bonus. Forgiving may well enable love diminished or obliterated by resentment to flourish again, and in life generally you feel more loving and lovable. Relief from the tension and pain of unforgiving-ness and the balm of love and positivity give your sense of wellbeing a huge boost and are good for your immune system, too.

Forgiveness and healers and their patients

Recently, there's been a surge in recognition of the importance of compassion shown by carers and healers. All of us who look after those who are ill in any way – doctors, nurses, paramedics and other carers – need to be aware of and practise the immensely valuable and therapeutic compassion that transforms medicine and home and community care.

Compassionate care makes a tremendous difference both to how patients feel and often to their physical symptoms and recovery. It's agreed by the UK's National Health Service and most doctors now that all medics should be taught and should practise the following tenets. This applies to all carers – that is, all of us – for we are all healers.

▶ Be aware of the pain and suffering of the patient (or the person you're caring for) and their accompanying worry and tension.

▶ Be as empathic as you can – imagining what it would be like to be that person. With a patient, it often helps to imagine how you would feel if they were your mother, child or other loved one.

▶ Lose any prejudice you may have: see beyond age, race, status and physical appearance. If you find you are reacting to them negatively, firmly make sure it doesn't influence your compassionate care.

▶ Show your compassion and empathy warmly; as well as in your words, it should be apparent in your eyes, your smile and your body language.

▶ Use all your senses to help consider their needs: giving them the opportunity to talk, asking the right questions, above all listening carefully to them.

Clear communication is also extremely therapeutic. Understanding what's happening increases our ability to cope with pain and symptoms and is a great aid to recovery.

> 'When doctors and nurses really sympathize with their patients, this is a drug more powerful and effective than all the drugs they give to them.'
>
> Prof. Dimitrios G. Oreopoulos, MD, Ph.D.

Focus points

✻ Positive feelings such as forgiveness, kindness and warmth towards others are healing and help us maintain good health, too.

✻ You can actively choose the attitude that helps create the 'feel-good' chemicals that promote wellbeing and good health.

✻ A forgiving attitude with compassion at its heart is important to all of us when caring for ourselves and others.

✻ Forgive someone – and notice the relief flowing through you and how much better you feel.

✻ A willingness to let go of big and small grievances is a vital elixir for our health.

✻ Positive thinking and constructive behaviour not only help us choose to let go of negative feelings, they take their place. And it feels good.

Next step

In Chapter 4, Making forgiveness your default setting, we'll look at how we can remember our wish to have a forgiving nature and return to the forgiving way whenever we stray into being critical.

Making forgiveness your default setting

In this chapter you will learn:

▶ *How developing forgiveness as a way of being can defuse all sorts of situations*

▶ *How to develop a more relaxed attitude in our relations with others*

▶ *The wisdom of Meister Eckhart.*

It's so easy to get riled. We may live permanently on a short fuse and assume it's part of our personality. Or we might put those times when we feel decidedly unforgiving down to a variety of other reasons – for instance being busy, feeling sensitive, not feeling well or just being plain tired.

For all of us life is full of incidents that are hurtful or annoying or have the potential to be. How we cope with them is individual and it's surprising how much leeway we have to choose the way we react. Some of us have the knack of staying as calm and non-judgemental as possible but another very common way of reacting to a perceived or real threat is to jump straight into aggressive or passive-aggressive mode that's out of all proportion.

You've been there? You pore over a problem and, whether it's real or imagined, the same thoughts scramble round and round in your mind, like a hamster on a wheel, to the whole or near exclusion of reason. This is not good for you or the others involved or the situation. For when we jump on our high horse like this we become blinded to other perspectives. It also obscures the good to be found if, instead, we're willing to open our eyes and hearts to it.

Most of us have experienced this feeling of self-righteous huffiness or outrage and obsessed about whatever wrong it is we think someone is doing us. Whether it's over something trivial or major, the energy you put into your unspoken inner diatribe (or, worse still, a voiced one) will be debilitating. It's the same with suppressed but still-simmering resentment. It obscures great portions of our perspective. It doesn't help in any way and stands to exacerbate tensions and misery.

Key idea

When you make a forgiving way your natural manner of being, always returning to it as a matter of course, life will be so much easier for you and for everyone with whom you come into contact. By choosing it as your default setting, you'll find that the downs of life are far less unsettling and when you are hurt you'll go almost automatically into recovery mode.

Case study: How Mary developed a default setting of forgiveness

Mary said: 'It happened just this morning – I was walking round the shops in my lunch hour obsessing about a disagreement I thought was going to blow up between me and a colleague. I suddenly thought, "What am I doing? This hasn't happened yet. I might have it wrong, or if we do disagree we can talk about it and sort it out. I won't let it spoil my leisure time – or any of my time, come to that."

'As it turned out, there was a problem and, at my suggestion, we discussed it calmly. It turned out we couldn't solve it ourselves so we agreed to ask our boss for an opinion. With her help we found a way forward. If I hadn't remembered my new default setting of forgivingness you encouraged me to make, we'd have squabbled and it would probably have blown up into a row!'

Because of Mary's quick decision to be pleasant and rational, she and her colleague were mutually civil, paid attention to each other's viewpoints and agreed to get help in finding the best way forward. A forgiving attitude paved the way to a good outcome. Mary added: 'When I was ranting on in my mind, I was even planning to hand in my notice! Thank goodness I came to my senses, realized what I was doing, calmed down and got my balance back.'

We can all use the points from Mary's experience to help us restore balance:

Try it now: Get some balance and perspective

1 Notice when you're obsessing or simmering about something.
2 Wait until you have all the facts – it may be that there is nothing out of order.
3 Forgive yourself for the aggressive feelings that were multiplying inside you. Shake your head with kindly disbelief that you were letting it spoil your happiness in the moment.
4 When the time comes, if there is something that needs attention, approach it with common sense as well as kindness, getting help as necessary.
5 Forgive others if they're being irrational – remember, you might have gone that route.
6 Help everyone get the situation into perspective and deal with it accordingly.

Choosing a relaxed attitude

It's great to able to cope with worries well. But even better is to pre-empt episodes of worry by taking a relaxed attitude to begin with. So, when an anxiety comes up, whether it's about someone's behaviour or something that might happen but hasn't yet, immediately pay attention to your concern and decide how you'll deal with it positively should it come about. Taking this relaxed view and realizing that it may not happen anyway is forgiving of any situation, and it's surprising how often it helps completely avoid an upset.

It's as though we radiate a healing, calming feeling that soothes everyone around us. People who are good with animals know that calm thoughts, fairness and kindness work wonders in gaining their trust and encouraging them to come to you and understand what you want from them. You'll find you'll have the same effect on people when you're calm, relaxed, fair and kind. Everyone relaxes and storm clouds move away of their own accord.

Acceptance

Acceptance is another powerful part of the forgiving way. So often we don't need to take issue, and wisdom is knowing when to just go along with what someone else says.

Case study: How David revealed the secret of happiness

A neighbour of mine was happily married for several decades and always spoke warmly and lovingly of his late wife. I asked him: 'What was the secret of your happiness together then, David?' He smiled with a twinkle in his eyes as he told me: 'Two words: "Yes, dear",' he said. Although amused, for a moment I worried that it meant he had given way to her or anyone else's every whim. But he quickly explained that so often there are times when it's easy and soothing to accept what's said without compromising our individuality, our rights or what is right. 'It's about being *agreeable*,' he stressed. 'It's as easy to be agreeable as it is to be disagreeable – and it feels better all round, doesn't it?'

I'm not recommending that you should be a 'yes person', but to realize that a lot of the time we don't have to rise to opportunities to argue or be difficult.

Key idea

There are always two ways we can answer or react, positively or negatively. So, even if we don't agree with what someone says or does, and feel we should or need to express this, there is probably a way to do so that's not inflammatory or antagonistic.

'Be a peacemaker,' Kay Potts, a nurse I worked with many years ago, used to advise. She was right – it's a good way of being.

Try it now: Think before you disagree

1 Next time someone says something and you're about to contradict them, pause and think.
2 Is it really necessary to wade in with an opposing opinion?
3 If so, aim for an interesting discussion rather than any kind of combative argument!
4 Consider whether their opinion is valid.
5 Can you learn something from it?

Serenity

Both David and Kay are great examples of serene beings. They were much loved and well respected for being as strong and wise as they were agreeable. There is something about serenity that shines out of the people who embrace it and affects everyone in their vicinity.

Remember this

The well-loved prayer attributed to Karl Paul Reinhold Niebuhr says it all:

'God, grant me the serenity to accept the things I cannot change,
The courage to change the things I can,
And wisdom to know the difference.'

This is another part of the forgiveness spectrum – a glowing, golden part.

Thankfulness

I love this word – it sounds as beautiful as all it represents, and it's another segment of the forgiveness spectrum.

When we are thankful for something, the appreciation seems to seep into our very being. It changes something in our presence so that our mood lightens instantly. It also catalytically improves our perspective. Suddenly, when you take a split second to think of something you're glad about, not only do you feel better but you see the futility of blaming and criticizing other people and moaning generally. And then – in that blissful reprieve – you suddenly see the truth of any situation that's been niggling or tormenting you, from all perspectives, clearly. It's a state of forgivingness – forgiving yourself for having been so ready to accuse and blame, and a readiness to forgive others should there be any reason to do so – though it's astonishing how often you see that there isn't.

'If the only prayer you ever say in your entire life is thank you, it will be enough.'

Meister Eckhart, German theologian

Meister Eckhart was right. It is enough. It changes everything and enables you to continue in your forgiving way of being.

1   To lighten and brighten a specific mood and situation, think of something that you are thankful for and give thanks.
2   To lighten and brighten your life generally, it's a great daily habit to write down some things you're glad about – one thing or lots of things.
3   Notice as the weeks go by how they come to mind increasingly, day by precious day.
4   Say thank you for this day in your life. Whatever it holds, the gift of life is a blessing. Be aware that you are much blessed.
5   Feel the gladness.

The power of silence – and graceful talk

Try it now: Listen, truly listen

1   Keep your antennae alert even when you're speaking.
2   How is the other person reacting?
3   Are they waiting to speak or frantically trying to get a word in?
4   Be aware of your tone, pitch and volume, too. If your voice is high-pitched or squeaky or anxious or, worst of all, you are shouting, you'll give the wrong impression and possibly intimidate or anger the other person. So, lower your voice and speak considerately and calmly.
5   Take care to speak at a reasonable pace, too – not too fast. Relax and the other person will relax as well.
6   Aim for all your words to be helpful and healing. It doesn't mean being boring! Wit and humour, intelligence and intellect can all shine through – just make sure your wit isn't wounding, your humour neither intentionally or casually hurtful, your intelligence and intellect free of any arrogance and not designed to diminish others.
7   Take turns in speaking and listening. But listen at least as much, if not more, than you speak.

If all this seems a lot to remember, the simplest key that covers it all is to remember that when we speak and listen we're communicating. Communicate kindly and you'll be fine.

Talking, of course, can be illuminating and can bridge the gap between you and another. But beware of angry talk and being so over-opinionated that your beliefs squash those of others. It's also all too easy to be so focused on what you're saying, and what you're about to say, that you drown out everyone and everything else.

Remember this

Only when we are silent can we listen. Only when we listen with our ears can we hear what someone is saying. Only when we listen with all our senses and our heart can we fully understand – and forgive.

Positivity and forgiveness

Choosing to think positively is transformational in so many ways, just as thankfulness is. There are always different ways to view something. How we perceive a person, their actions or the situation can change dramatically if we change from a negative approach to a positive one. It doesn't mean saying 'yes' to something when we really don't want to or when it wouldn't be wise. A refusal and the word 'no' may be the right, positive decision for you if they are the result of positive, clear thought and followed by a willingness to look for a positive outcome or way forward.

People have often spoken of the way that holding on to a positive thought or memory has helped them survive the bleakest of circumstances and live the rest of their life in light rather than be affected for ever by the darkness they've witnessed and experienced. We'll look at this more in Chapter 16, Trauma and forgiveness. It's helpful to be mindful of this here because if positivity and a forgiving attitude help in the abyss of desolation, just think of its tremendous power in our everyday lives. That power is effective in every walk of life, every situation, in every personality.

Key idea

To think positively is to seek a good way to do whatever we are doing well. It's the encouraging, inspiring way to help others, a kind way to comfort and console. And it's the way to forgive or to accept forgiveness.

Remember this

Refusing to be treated badly and putting up sensible boundaries are not negative but positive – and help you live forgivingly. They also reinforce your inner strength.

Even when the situation is extremely sensitive and difficult – especially then – you can choose to remember your default setting of forgiveness and let positivity flow through you, and when you do you walk in the way of forgiveness.

With the forgiving way as your default setting, you will find that you refer to it all the time.

Try it now: 'What is the best thing I can do?'

A simple way to find out is to think in any potentially or actively difficult or sensitive situation: 'What is the best thing to do?' Sometimes the answer won't come immediately, in which case be prepared to wait before speaking or acting.

* See if you can intuit the underlying currents of the situation.
* Consider if you need to do some research.
* Reconnect with your natural kindness.
* Check that you're not being self-righteous! Living the forgiving way is about being aware that we are all fallible human beings and that we have no right to feel or act as though we're superior.
* Consider whether there's any need to be anything other than compassionate to the best of your ability.

This mode of being is soothing for ourselves and others. It's the way of calm – forgiveness in flow.

Focus points

✻ Living on a short fuse is a habit that's a hindrance to happiness. Instead, we can transform our lives by quickly getting the annoyance into perspective and then either letting it go or dealing with it calmly and constructively.

✻ Forgive others if they're irritable and help them do the same.

✻ Be a peacemaker and see the beneficial effect you have on situations.

✻ Accept what you can't change, change what should and can be changed, and seek the wisdom to know the difference!

✻ Every day be thankful for your blessings – it will light up your day.

Next step

In Chapter 5, Forgiveness and communication, we'll look at how we can understand each other better by communicating and how it helps us and others live forgivingly.

Forgiveness and communication

In this chapter you will learn:

▶ *How good communication skills underpin living the forgiving way*

▶ *How communicating as honestly and with as much clarity as possible can enable us to understand and forgive... and be forgiven*

▶ *How modern communication methods such as email and social networking can lead to misunderstanding and offence.*

Key idea

When we communicate positively our spirits touch and forgiveness flows between us.

It is impossible to overestimate the value of good communication. It opens windows of understanding, knowledge and freedom and builds bridges when we're feeling confused or estranged. It defuses tension and diffuses light, simultaneously softening, clarifying and brightening. It makes living forgivingly much easier.

When we exchange information about ourselves, it helps us understand each other's character, feelings and needs. Mutual understanding can seem magically transmitted and may well be due to an element of intuition, but mostly it's learned by what we reveal to each other through our self-presentation, body language and, most of all, what we say and how we say it.

The word 'communicate' itself is brilliant at revealing its meaning. *Com* means 'with' and the key root *mun* is related in meaning to munificence, community and communion, a close or spiritual association. Let's just think, then, of how good it would be if we all communicated with each other meaningfully and generously, with the wish to empathize with each other and exchange useful information. We would then be part of the same community, for we are all human beings sharing the same world and needing to live forgivingly and caringly.

If we communicate well, we immediately cut out much of the confusion and misunderstanding that cause problems in relationships of all kinds. When everyone knows exactly where they are with you and the situation, discussion is easier, solutions and compromises negotiable. Democracy is based on good communication. It helps us respect and look out for each other. It helps the union between two people in any relationship. It also helps create accord between millions around the world (more of that in Chapter 21, World forgiveness.

Communication is an individual recipe – we have our own ways of relating and speaking, but as long as we are truthful, and at the same time sensitive to others' feelings, the words will come out right. When we communicate caringly we preclude hurtful situations.

Knowing what you want to say and talk about in a potentially sensitive or difficult situation

How talking about our feelings helps us recover and take the forgiving road

When we tell someone sensitive and caring how we are feeling – *really* feeling – they lift some of the burden of these feelings from us. It may be just a temporary sharing during the time we are communicating with them, but it can make a great difference to how we cope.

It's difficult, however, to let your feelings flow if you're not used to talking at this depth about such things.

Try it now: Let your feelings flow

To help you let go of inhibitions about expressing your feelings, talk to a friend or someone else you trust implicitly – perhaps a minister or someone else whose wisdom you respect and whom you like as well. It's important that they are also generally positive about life and don't have a tendency to be critical and unforgiving of others.

Remember that he or she may not be used to listening for long periods, so accept it if they want to voice their thoughts, too. Feelings they've had and personal disclosures of similar experiences they've come through may reveal ways to help you through yours.

However, it's also good to have someone who will simply listen to you empathically as you recount what's happened and your past and present feelings. Your doctor or local community centre can refer you to an experienced counsellor.

As well as, or instead of, talking to someone, you may find it very therapeutic to write about what's happened and your feelings in a journal that no one else will read. Don't edit your thoughts – let them flow across the paper. Thoughts dropped on to paper in this way are like tears flowing and, especially when real tears join them, it can give a huge sense of pain being washed clean and, afterwards, a welcome sense of relief and healing.

Expressing our feelings can be a valuable part of healing along the way of forgiving.

Expressing our negative feelings lets them flow so they don't get stale or impacted within us. It also helps us learn from them, get the situation in perspective, deal with it practically, and move forwards constructively and forgivingly.

Communicating through modern technology

The communications industry offers us a positive banquet of ways to communicate. The more we communicate lovingly, clearly, helpfully and compassionately the better. The minute we forget this good intention, we put ourselves in potentially grave danger.

When you're with someone, you read the other person's eyes, facial expressions and body language and, if you're especially intuitive, you may also pick up on their aura, the atmosphere around them that radiates their inner being – how they really, really are. But when you're texting, emailing and even speaking on the phone, you miss out on all this and it's incredibly easy to misunderstand. It's also so easy to fire off messages at the touch of a button before we've really thought out how we feel, what we want to say, how to put it across well and how to communicate in the forgiving way – compassionately and clearly.

The smallest things can be misinterpreted – the insensitive use of an emoticon, the number or lack of 'x's and so on. You may come across as glib or over-intense or inappropriate. You may mistakenly lead someone on or otherwise give them the wrong impression. You may – especially on social media – get carried away and show off, to the detriment of a friend, thereby severely offending them.

When I was a girl a wise friend of my parents with a brilliant mind and a great sense of humour was careful never to use his gifts against someone. He told me: 'Always be careful who you are facetious with.' We forget it at our peril whenever we're with others, but his timeless advice is never more apt than when using modern technology. We all need to watch out for foolish, inappropriate, ill-timed or ill-judged thoughts and remarks. Transmitted in a nanosecond, they can cool or even destroy relationships.

Remember this

It only takes a few moments longer to check that the message we're about to deliver is in the forgiving spectrum, that it's thoughtful, warm and clear.

Checking out our own perspective with someone wise

I have a friend who spent her legal career doing her best for her clients but at the same time trying to ensure that they could see their situation clearly and in the round. If I'm aware that I'm wound up about something, obsessing extremely emotionally one way or another, I'll call her and ask: 'Is this rational and reasonable, or am I out of order or being neurotic?'

There is probably someone in your circle who can do the same for you by looking objectively at the situation and helping you get a fresh perspective that enables you to think of a more positive way forward than eating yourself up with anger and bitterness. It also helps us spot our own righteous indignation that perhaps isn't as righteous as we first thought.

This friend, like mine, will:

▶ help you assess – usually within a few minutes – whether you need to calm down completely and drop the issue or channel the emotion into a constructive plan to resolve the situation as positively as possible

▶ remind and help you to be compassionate, truthful and fair

▶ help you, when apt, to put up firm boundaries or draw closure

▶ help you to keep walking the forgiving way.

Remember this

Choose the friends you communicate with about serious personal matters very carefully. Avoid anyone who encourages you to criticize, hate, blame and be unforgiving. Choose someone who helps you to think clearly but positively, compassionately and constructively.

Talking also helps us to think of how we can deal with things when something terrible has happened that we absolutely can't fathom. Whenever I've talked this over with others, we've come to the same conclusion: letting the horror of it pull us into a deep depression or enflame negative emotions is detrimental to our own lives and the lives of those around us. Of course, we mustn't be dismissive or blasé about what has happened, but only by refusing to let it bring us down, and instead finding something constructive, atoning or otherwise positive about it, can we hope to fight the evil it sows. Love is stronger than hate; good vanquishes evil; positivity overcomes negativity. Forgiveness in any of its many ways brings healing.

Remember this

Your spirit is immensely strong – all it needs to keep burning strong within you is your willingness to recognize it and let it be there for you at all times. Look to positive people to discuss these things with – with your mutual positivity you will help each other follow the forgiving way.

The thought of being able to forgive someone might seem like a miracle that's never going to happen. Actually the miracle is already here, waiting for you to step into, and often we suddenly realize this as we're talking or otherwise communicating with someone. Expressing our thoughts and feelings – our version of events – to someone we trust confirms that our bereavement and grief are real, unavoidable emotions, as are anger and all the other negative emotions in the aftermath of hurt, loss and trauma. They are normal and natural and help us endure and in time get through what's happened.

Key idea

Dialogue also helps us arrive at a place of catharsis. We realize that, if we dwell too long in negative feelings, they can seem insurmountable and hope of recovery seems an illusion. But when we decide to accept the possibility of healing and forgiving we enable ourselves to keep going through even the worst of times.

We have choices to help us get through difficult times. They are compassion, kindness, understanding or any of the other forgiving ways we've talked about; they are there at your fingertips for you to use. They will heal you and free you from hate, and, free of hate and desperation, you will walk the real way of healing and forgiving. Good friends and wise counsellors will help you with this and, in time, help you reinstate your inner peace. It is there for you, waiting.

Focus points

✳ Communicating honestly and clearly helps us understand each other and be forgiving.

✳ When we're authentic and have integrity we are so much more likely to live in harmony, walking the forgiving way.

✳ Talking about your problems helps you heal. It often shows you how to solve them, too.

✳ Expressing negative feelings helps prevent them simmering away, impacted within you.

✳ Modern technology is brilliant for communication, but remember to use it thoughtfully and wisely.

→ **Next step**

In Chapter 6, Healing discord with a forgiving way, we will explore in more detail how a forgiving attitude and approach can heal conflict of various kinds.

Healing discord with a forgiving way

In this chapter you will learn:

▶ *How to discuss an issue constructively without the danger of it escalating into a row*

▶ *How to complain – the forgiving way*

▶ *How to criticize someone without offending.*

Connection with others is the heartbeat of the soul, love in its many forms its lifeblood and communication its circulation. The vital ingredient that keeps love and connection flowing and our communication meaningful, positive and rewarding is forgiveness. Day by day, remembering to be kind, compassionate and supportive – all part of the forgiving way of life – keeps our relationships free of damaging conflict and a warm, healthy and pleasant place to be.

Relationships of all kinds are vulnerable to the effects of negative behaviour, though, and when we forget to be forgiving it's very easy to find ourselves unsettling, needling or directly hurting the people in our lives. If a propensity to upset our relationships goes unchecked, it's liable to become a malign and infectious habit that does no one any good.

In this chapter we'll look at the ways we can hinder and spoil our rapport with others and how a forgiving way helps us avoid doing this. Then in Chapter 10, Forgiveness in relationships, we will focus on the different kinds of relationship to see how forgiveness can more specifically help.

Arguing

In relationships, the most common interaction that cries out for forgiveness is an argument that spirals out of control. A difference of opinion needn't cause friction and can be thought-provoking, but becomes destructive as soon as we entrench ourselves in our opinions. Then, all too easily, even the nicest, normally most rational of people can turn into tyrants obsessed with having their own way and/or bullies who try to bludgeon the other person with words into changing their mind and agreeing. It feels and sounds horrible when this happens. When an argument gets out of control, we may speak angrily, autocratically, pompously or whiningly and what we say is likely to become increasingly hurtful.

Let's look at the chain of events we can set in progress when we argue aggressively about a difference of opinion instead of discussing it civilly:

▶ We disagree.

▶ We become defensive.

- Chemicals start to affect our brains preparing us for conflict.

- We start to take whatever's being said extremely personally.

- We argue more vociferously and perhaps aggressively.

- The chemicals are now in full flood, causing uncomfortable emotions.

- We probably become irrational or at least exaggerate.

- However the argument finishes, we are both left with a decidedly uncomfortable feeling that may spoil the rest of the day if untended.

Now let's look at a better way.

It helps to remember that we may *both* be right and to be ready, always, to listen to each other and consider each other's points calmly and fully. Arguing our differing views can be thought-provoking and illuminating and doesn't have to be damaging at all, as long as we are resolutely respectful of each other and each other's views. 'Ah!' – you may say – 'but then it would be a discussion rather than an argument.'

It's all a matter of degree. Defending our views, discussing, debating – all these are stimulating and potentially useful in widening our knowledge and stretching our capacity to think. This kind of arguing is beneficial because we can learn and perhaps discover another truth. Indeed, there is a famous quote, from Marie von Ebner-Eschenbach, stating that: 'Whenever two good people argue over principles, they are both right.' However, the opposite is also true: a friend of mine remembers that his grandmother embroidered a cushion with this alternative thought: 'When two people argue they are both wrong.' We may, of course, find that there is some right *and* wrong in what we are each saying. And perhaps Ebner-Eschenbach meant that taking the time and thought to argue over principles is always right in that it's useful and may lead to and increase wisdom. Certainly, though, when argument descends through the downward spiral noted above, it's wrong and damaging for everyone involved.

Key idea

We're bound to disagree about things because we all have minds and opinions of our own. The forgiving way that pre-empts arguments becoming spiteful and perhaps developing into rows is to discuss rather than argue. We're all tempted to do all these things because we're not perfect. But, oh, it makes life so much easier if we can be aware of the tendency and guard against it with shields of steel.

Try it now: Talk constructively

* In a way, it's about forgiving as we go. How much better it is to follow this path when you disagree with someone.
* Instead of becoming defensive, remember that you both may have a point and it's worth listening to each other.
* Be aware that your defensive/aggressive chemicals are on standby, ready to create havoc if you get angry at being disagreed with. So refuse to take what the other is saying personally. Remember that this is a rational discussion and should not be a personal attack on you or by you.
* Talk together about your differing views and see if you can bridge them. Is there a possible compromise or a way of one accommodating the other more easily?
* Be kind and polite to each other.
* Don't let your heightened emotions channel you into exaggeration or irrationality
* When you're done discussing, say, as appropriate, 'Good, that's decided then' or 'Let's agree to differ and see if we can think it through logically and choose by mutual agreement the best route forward or compromise.'
* If, despite your best efforts at keeping calm, you are left with residual frustration and you keep replaying the disagreement in your mind, do something constructive or healing like phoning the other person and being kind – for instance offering help with something unrelated.
* If they are with you, give them a hug. It will show that you're not taking it personally and that you hope they're not either.
* If during the discussion you said anything hurtful or otherwise out of order, apologize for it.

Your recognition of any points on which you agree and the way you voice them can be catalytic in defusing rancour. You could say, for example, 'I understand why you think this,' or you could ask a question and carefully listen to their answer, showing that you respect what they're saying even if you disagree with it. Speaking kindly, perhaps imagining a loving atmosphere around you both, is even more effective.

> 'I disapprove of what you say, but I will defend to the death your right to say it.'
>
> Beatrice Evelyn Hall's summary of the approach of 18th-century philosopher Voltaire

On the compromising front, positive questions and suggestions are helpful, so be ready to ask: 'How about we do so and so?' or 'How could we get round this or come up with a satisfactory solution for both of us?' or 'Let's brainstorm this and find a different path that takes us both forwards in a good way.'

Listen! We all love to be paid attention to – it's fundamental to our wellbeing, so listen carefully and thoughtfully.

Complaining

We've all met people whose modus operandi is complaining. Their conversation is peppered or suffused with all kinds of complaints or a few they focus on. We may find ourselves joining in, nodding sagely in agreement and, by adding our moans, fuelling the negative atmosphere. This is a real downer. But often we get so carried away with the collusion that we don't notice that it doesn't feel so good. Make a point of noticing. Be aware of how moaning is affecting your mind, body and soul. Just writing about it I feel it tightening the muscles across my back and see clearly the sad facial expressions and taut or slumped body language of the participants in any complaining chorus.

There's a better, forgiving way – you'll be well aware of it, I expect, but it's surprising how easy it is, nevertheless, to get caught up in a binge of complaint. Like avoiding most bad habits, it's essential to recognize the symptoms the minute we're in danger of being sucked into the cycle and consciously and determinedly take a different path.

Try it now: How to avoid grumbling

1 Notice complaining – not just open, obvious grumbling but any degree of whingeing. It could be you or the other person expressing a grievance. Just be aware of the complaining nature or tone of the conversation.

2 Pay the subject of the dissatisfaction the attention it deserves.

3 Then acknowledge that you are aware that there's a danger of getting stuck in a groove – you could say, for instance, 'Hey – enough moaning' or 'Rant over!'

4 Say something positive on the subject if you wish. It helps to take a step back for a moment to think forgivingly about whomever the moan is directed at. This doesn't necessarily mean letting them off the hook if the criticism is deserved (see the section on complaining effectively and forgivingly below); it means being fair and compassionate. They are a human being, remember, just like you.

5 Now change the subject to one that you can be positive about and resolve not to descend into any more negativity.

Sometimes we *need* to speak out and complain. Being a doormat only encourages thoughtless or abusive people to continue to walk over us or treat us poorly. But there is no need to depress ourselves by indulging in a dirge of complaints, whether it's in our own minds or among friends. The forgiving way is instead to do something constructive about it – expressing our views clearly to whoever's responsible with suggestions for how they could improve. When given the chance and encouragement to do better, it's surprising how often people do so.

Can complaint be made in a forgiving way? Absolutely – and you're much more likely to get a good result when you do so. The alternative, to complain forcefully and angrily, floods the other person and the ground between you with negativity that will probably serve only to make them react defensively and contentiously.

When someone's behaviour gives you real reason, you feel, to complain, it's a good idea to get reassurance that you're not being pernickety but have a valid point by bouncing the situation off someone who can give you advice from a different perspective. Wise friends will do this for each other.

Try it now: How to complain – the forgiving way

Outline the situation to a sensible friend. Ask: 'Am I being touchy or awkward, or do I have reason to be concerned/irritated/upset about this? Should I say something?' If they agree you have reason to ask for change, do so politely and clearly along the following lines:

1 If the person is sensitive and normally considerate, a gentle suggestion may be all it takes to draw their attention to your concern and bring about a change of behaviour.
2 If your subtle approach isn't noticed, then voice exactly what's bugging you and the change you'd like to see.
3 Speak courteously and calmly.
4 Don't whinge or criticize.
5 Don't use the point you're making as an excuse to bring up old grievances or dive into a character assassination.

If approached calmly and pleasantly, most people are readily willing to take on board a suggestion that their behaviour has left something to be desired and are keen to rectify it. However, it may take a few hours or a day or two for them to process their reaction – after all, receiving a complaint, however peaceably delivered, is never pleasant. So give them time.

With any luck, there'll be no need to bring it up again, but, if you do, again be calm and clear in stating the outcome you'd like to see. As we saw in the section on arguing, looking for something you can agree about or a mutually satisfactory compromise may orientate them towards being helpful.

Kindness, understanding and enabling them to feel good about themselves will also help keep the interaction between you positive and friendly.

Criticizing

However, in recent years criticism has come to mean something that many fear because they've grown used to the harsh nature of so much criticism. Much of this dread of negative criticism stems from our work and our relationships with employers, managers and even our peers. It's also common in other relationships, so much so that many think it's acceptable to be negatively critical, either face to face or by criticizing others behind their backs. Negative criticism is as common as arguing and, like argument, damaging to your rapport, whether it's just a one-off or persistent.

Remember this

It's a measure of the prevalence of negative criticism that it's often assumed that criticism can only be negative and unforgiving. It needn't be, though – it can be an evaluation, opinion, commentary or critique of any kind.

The forgiving way turns this around and has the opposite effect. Instead of *going* in with a verbal knife to deliberately or casually cause pain and diminish confidence, you use words to lift the other person in some way. Give praise and other positive comments and compliments whenever you can, and helpful, positive thoughts when apt – all these help people tremendously and help us interact forgivingly in mutual compassion, kindness, encouragement ... and, of course, love.

In *The Prophet*, his collection of essays published in 1923, the Lebanese artist and poet Khalil Gibran recommends supporting our loved ones by encouraging them to be the best, truest person they can be. This is marvellous advice – and it doesn't only work in romantic and family relationships; it works wonders across all kinds of relationships.

Remember this

Every time you interact with someone, think about how your behaviour – what you say, your body language, your warmth and understanding – can affect them beneficially.

Remember this

When, without being unaware or naïve, you treat others forgivingly – that is kindly, encouragingly and compassionately – you open the door for them to behave well too.

Taking responsibility

When there's discord in any relationship, it's tempting to blame the other person for it. We might use inflammatory statements such as: 'It wasn't *my* fault', 'She started it' or 'He's so unreasonable.' Or we might cast ourselves as a victim of the other's short fuse or lack of understanding, and/or we might act like martyrs, making it obvious that we think we have the moral high ground. Whenever one or more of these is the case, for us to forgive might be patronizing and unjust.

Key idea

To be fair and truly forgiving, most times we need to own up to our part in the development of the disagreement. Saying sorry will invite the other person to apologize, too. It's like holding your hand out to clasp theirs, make up and either find a better way forward in a spirit of compromise or agree to differ and work, amicably, around that.

NOT PRESSING BUTTONS...

When we know someone well or are perceptive even of those we don't, it can be tempting, in the middle of an argument or just when we happen to feel out of sorts, to hurt them by using subtle triggers. We 'press their buttons' by mentioning something that will remind them of a past hurt or insecurity. Often, if challenged, we'll say 'I didn't mean that' or 'It was the last thing on my mind' or 'Don't take it so personally' when actually, if we're honest, we did mean it and it was personal. True, it may have been unconscious, but if so we need, then, to be even more watchful of what we're about to say. When we get the nearly irresistible urge to rile someone this way, we should resist it with every fibre of our being.

...AND NOT REACTING WHEN SOMEONE ELSE PRESSES YOURS

You'll know it when it happens: suddenly, or with gradually dawning awareness, you'll feel uncomfortable as though you're under attack, even though the person you're with is smiling and outwardly being nice. There is a forgiving way to handle it.

Try it now: How to defuse a personal attack

1 Face them with what they're doing by saying – warmly and politely but nevertheless firmly – something like 'Hey – you're pressing my buttons. Is it unconscious?' or 'What's the matter – did something happen to make you unhappy?' Having the playing field levelled in this way will likely fluster them but also enable them to recognize their irritation, whatever it may be, and let it flow out of them.

2 Give them time to recompose themselves by getting on with whatever you're doing and determinedly not taking whatever they've said or done say personally. Not reacting to needling by lashing back angrily is forgiveness in action. It enables them to take the time they need to recognize what they were doing and drop it.

3 If they can't drop it and again needle you, you could say gently but firmly: 'I don't have to accept this.' This way you're reacting forgivingly from the start, so that, unreciprocated, their needling can't upset you or escalate into a row.

Being given firm boundaries is as good for all of us as it is for children and teenagers. When aspects of life, whether it's hormones or trouble at work, make us inwardly fractious and we start to take it out on others, especially perhaps our loved ones, we will at some level feel bad about it. A boundary, whether imposed by them or ourselves, is actually welcome. The space afforded by your or their refusal to be hurt or enter into a sparring match is also valuable – it gives much-needed time to relax and remember that actually this person isn't the one you need to take issue with but a friend and ally. The forgiveness passes between you – healing, soothing, mending.

An important note on mind games and verbal and physical abuse

Some people take needling and all forms of verbally hurting others a stage further, playing games, twisting conversations and being verbally abusive in all kinds of other ways through to direct cruelty. As with physical abuse, they'll make out it's your fault, then, when they've succeeded in infuriating, confusing and/or attacking and hurting you, apologize profusely and promise it won't happen again.

Verbal abuse is insidious and, sadly, increasingly prevalent in our society. It may be caused by mental illness, personality disorder and/or alcoholism or another addiction, and forgiveness alone is unlikely to help the abuser as they need help in understanding and stopping their extremely damaging behaviour. This is a complex subject and needs specialist help. In the case of verbal abuse I recommend visiting the website that expertly addresses this: www.verbalabuse.com. For physical abuse, which *under no circumstances* must be tolerated, telephone in the UK 0808 2000 247 or visit www.nationaldomesticviolencehelpline.org.uk. In the United States, telephone the National Domestic Violence Hotline on 1-800-799-7233 or visit www.thehotline.org/help/

With any kind of abuse, it's imperative that you protect yourself and seek experienced help.

! Focus points

* Rather than arguing, which can so easily escalate into a row, listen, talk, discuss and see whether you can find some common ground and compromise or solution. If not, agree to disagree.
* Realize that other people are free to have their own ideas and views.
* If you need to take a stand, do it as positively and constructively as possible. Encourage rather than criticize, think of a better way forward rather than complain. Be ready to seek expert help.
* Behave well and you'll encourage others to behave forgivingly, too – that is, kindly, compassionately, encouragingly.
* Don't knowingly press other people's buttons, and, if they press yours, don't rise to it. Try to understand what's going on in either case and, in doing so, you'll probably be able to defuse the tension.

→ Next step

In Chapter 7, Where forgiveness can work wonders, we'll look at the often astonishing way a forgiving attitude can soothe hurt and fears, and at how, even in the most difficult of situations, it can make a beneficial difference.

Where forgiveness can work wonders

In this chapter you will learn:

▶ *How we can avoid violence and seek out peace*

▶ *How we can turn prejudice into tolerance*

▶ *How we can make good our mistakes, or, if this is impossible, atone for them*

▶ *A simple yet wonderful technique for finding calm.*

Fraught and unhappy situations of all kinds usually harbour blame and resentment at their centre. They reek with a toxic brew of shame, fear, aggression, and/or defensiveness – psychological webs of stretched or tortured nerves. As well as being hell for the chief protagonists, the strands spin out to affect other people, other relationships. So often everyone turns a blind eye to it as though it's somehow easier to ignore it than face up to and do something about it. Yet the web of unforgiving is pervasive and pernicious, and can become deadly poisonous, not just to the wrongdoers, but to the ones who have been hurt and anyone they're close to. For bitterness affects everyone in the vicinity and its intrinsic nature is to damage.

Awareness, openness to healing, on the other hand, can start a transformation. A simple impulse to forgive or show compassion, or even just the thought of doing so, lights a candle of hope. Found on the headstone of a Jewish Holocaust victim are these beautiful words: 'All the darkness in the world could not put out the light of one small candle.' This is a simple and immensely powerful truth. The light of forgiveness illuminates, heals, allows learning, encourages wisdom. It shows up prejudice, violence, unkindness. It enables us to keep going, to keep our sanity, to keep the flame of our soul alight.

We can all make a difference and shine the light of forgiveness, somehow, somewhere. Let's look at some of the circumstances where forgiveness, in some measure, can offer you a lifeline. As you think of some of the areas which could be lit up and healed, listen to your heart and soul – how can *you* shine a light to lighten the darkness?

The media: from violence to peace

Much of the wrongdoing that abounds in every society, both in private and public life, is due to ignorance. People don't think through the impact that their behaviour will have and are unaware of the extent to which empathy and understanding, as the very starting point of getting on with our fellow human beings, would be the outstandingly better option. It's often been argued that there is no excuse for ignorance and that's never been truer than today when we have literally at our fingertips access to a world of experience and research. We can find out about, and be inspired by, human interaction, forgiveness and the peace process, reminding us that we too can transfuse our and others' lives with wellbeing, harmony and love. And, if more and more of us do the same, just think how it will help grow and hasten progress towards world peace.

Yet it's so easy to waste time watching violence in the media or, worse still, engaging with it as though it were a computer game. It's the same with 'celebrity gossip' that even broadsheet newspapers and quality broadcasters such as the BBC clearly believe they have to feed us. And yet these things don't make us feel good or forgiving.

Let's vow, right now, to resist them firmly more and more and enjoy the surprising pleasure of seeking out dramas, documentaries and books that teach us something about the things that are crucial to our survival as a civilization and as happy, fulfilled individuals. Let's soak up stories of kindness, truth, honour of the best sort, compassion and all the wonderful positive traits of human beings that illuminate the darkness of the worst sides of our natures and encourage compassion and peace. (There's more on this in Chapter 13, Forgiveness and the power of stories and music.)

> 'Out of clutter, find simplicity. From discord, find harmony. In the middle of difficulty, lies opportunity.'
>
> Albert Einstein

Try it now: Resist media violence and small-mindedness

✻ Say no to gratuitous violence in dramas – write to producers and directors to encourage them to leave it out.

✻ Say no to gratuitous spitefulness by newspaper columnists or bloggers – write to editors to say we've had enough.

✻ Tell both that what we do want is inspiration to enjoy life to the full, and encouragement to find resolution to problems and ways forward out of misfortune.

From making mistakes to putting things right or atoning for our mistakes

We all make mistakes and most of us have taken wrong turnings in life that have led us to behave badly. The minute we acknowledge such slip-ups, we create opportunities to remedy the situation in some way. Sometimes, if we're fortunate, we can act constructively to put things right. Most people forgive easily if the wrong is righted this way. And it helps us to let go of residual guilt and forgive ourselves, too.

If the damage cannot be repaired, the old-fashioned concept of atonement can be very helpful and can again pave the way for the person we've harmed to forgive us. Atoning for our wrongdoing means making up for it in some way, for instance doing something helpful for the person or for the community – something that will be appreciated, something that takes your time and effort.

Key idea

Atonement is a way of restoring the balance in the wake of harm and, although it won't remove the damage, it can at least take the sting out of it and soothe the person's anger. It's a kind of self-imposed justice.

Both mending damage we've caused and atoning for it make us feel better about ourselves, too, as well as (often) enabling the person to forgive us or at least to let go of continuing fear, anger and/or resentment.

From bad behaviour to thoughtfulness

Learning from our mistakes is helpful across the whole spectrum of forgiveness.

Remember this

When you learn something about your nature and deepen your understanding of why and how you're liable to behave badly, you greatly increase your ability to say no to such behaviour in future. In effect, we protect ourselves and others from repeating the bad behaviour.

Taking this journey from careless mistakes that cause harm to deliberate thoughtfulness that helps us avoid doing harm inevitably means we mature and grow into more rounded and balanced beings. It helps us take a place in communities – in relationships, families, at work and generally out and about in society. When we're thoughtful of others and careful of the way we interact with them, we relate to them better. It feels more comfortable. It means we can go about our lives without treading on people's feet or, indeed, having them tread on ours.

So much in life is about balance and thought, and the two together usually pre-empt wrongdoing in the first place and also, therefore, the need for forgiveness.

From unkindness to kindness

It's frighteningly easy to be unkind. A sharp word, a sarcasm that, however funny, is always cutting, an inconsiderate action – all can come about in an instant. All can cut to the quick and be very difficult to forgive and forget.

Today's culture encourages unkindness. Satirical shows, caustic judging panels, journalists vying with each other to be as mean as possible – all appear to tell us that it's acceptable to be unkind. It isn't. Ever. It's hurtful and can be dangerous. It's no good saying to someone caustically 'Get over it!', as though they are somehow at fault for being hurt by a nasty remark or action. Any unkindness may have lasting damage – sometimes causing pain and having a detrimental effect on the person's path or self-confidence for decades.

One of the saddest things I've heard over and over as an agony aunt and counsellor is the deepest regret when someone tells me, following a loved one's death: 'I said something horrible – if only I hadn't. If only I could have our time together over again and not say anything unkind.'

The truth is that it's just as easy to be kind. Then there's no need for forgiveness on either part and only mutual love and respect. Of course, we're not perfect and sometimes something unkind may slip out despite our best intentions, but as long as we're mostly kind and caring, forgiveness on these rare occasions will come spontaneously and probably almost instantly.

🕐 Try it now: Be kind

1 Just for today, resolve not to do anything unkind.
2 Monitor humour for any potentially hurtful sharpness or sarcasm.
3 Cut out negative criticism.
4 See how many kind things you can say and do for others.
5 Notice how often this requires you to forgive them for past grievances.
6 Be glad that you do.
7 Be glad that you are being/have been kind.
8 Notice how good it feels.

From insensitivity to sensitivity

Human nature gives us sensitivity in varying degrees. Some are born with personalities that predispose them to be thoughtful of others and naturally empathic and caring; others are simply not so spontaneously understanding of others' feelings and are reliant on nurture and, later, interaction with others to help them learn to be more sensitive and considerate. Many sadly slip through the net – they don't get the help they need to develop this aspect of their character from their parents and teachers or from the good example set by friends.

Understanding this lack of emotional intelligence in someone who hurts us can be hugely helpful in letting go of our indignation and disappointment. Being prepared to lead by example or by talking about such things could help them improve their social caring and understanding skills. There is always room for development; even the most crass, uncaring people can have a sea change and turn their lives around from disdain for others' feelings to genuine care and concern. Realizing this possibility and being prepared to cheer them on as they develop greater social and emotional awareness and intelligence makes it easier for us to live with their deficiency and continue to be sensitive, aware and caring ourselves – to be forgiving, to walk alongside them in hope.

From prejudice to openness

It's horrible being prejudiced. It makes us pompous and dogmatic – neither of which feel good. It makes others fear, pity or shy away from us – and that's unpleasant, too. And of course any misconception prejudice causes is likely to be hurtful to others and may be lethal.

As with all wrongdoing, the first step to stopping it is to realize that we're doing it, recognize the foolishness of it and the damage it could do.

Try it now: How to avoid prejudice

1 Next time you catch yourself feeling prejudiced, say to yourself: 'Hey – that's prejudice talking!'
2 Notice how this immediately opens the door to clear, unbiased thought.
3 Forgive yourself for the initial impulse to think, speak or act in a prejudiced way.
4 Be aware how this forgiveness gives you a lovely feeling of self-healing.
5 Notice how it also enables you to see the world in true perspective, free of the fog of bigotry.
6 From now on, determine to form your opinions based on current reality rather than prejudice.

Whole cultures and nations have developed deep-seated prejudices over the last few centuries and are continuing to do so in this one. We need to keep up the fight against prejudice and can start by banishing it from our own heads.

From distress and trauma to calm and healing

We'll be addressing stress and anxiety of many kinds throughout this book and looking at how forgiveness heals and helps. For now, try the following exercise.

It may sound childlike, but it works amazingly well. I'm smiling as I write this, remembering the first time I tried this technique after reading about it in *Living in the Light* by Shakti Gawain. A friend of mine who reads prolifically – novels and non-fiction – says that, while she rarely falls entirely for a book, in almost every one she reads she'll come across a nugget of gold. It could be an inspiration, a truth, something that makes her smile – but always something helpful that in some way lights up her life. Coming across the bubble exercise was such a find, and throughout my life ever since it's been astonishingly therapeutic in helping me to let go of stress and the accompanying feelings of resentment.

From resentment to acceptance

Often, becoming physically aware of how the various issues causing resentment are affecting each of you brings about a natural change in attitude, allowing you to relax, forgive yourselves and each other, and work out a way to get on better.

Acceptance can also be the answer when we can't shift resentment, no matter how much we want to. Part of a much-loved prayer puts this so well (we looked at this in Chapter 1):

'God, grant me the serenity to accept the things
I cannot change,
The courage to change the things I can,
And the wisdom to know the difference.'

Forgiveness is at the heart of this.

From irritation to tolerance

One friend of mine is very easily irritated. 'Do I irritate you?' I asked him one day. 'Yes, you do,' he said and added, 'Everybody irritates me!' Most of us aren't quite so easily riled, thankfully, but however accepting of others' foibles we are there are bound to be times in life when we are.

A wise teacher once told me a great way of resolving this problem. He said: 'First of all, let yourself off the hook. These things happen. But you can do something positive about it. Look for what's good about her. And, instead of being hostile, befriend her, being truly pleasant and helpful.'

This advice, passed on by me, has helped many others dissolve their irritation with someone in their life. It boils down to acceptance that these feelings can well up spontaneously and that doing something positive and constructive allows them to fall away again. Interestingly and pleasingly, very often the people concerned forge a strong friendship.

Yet again, acceptance and forgiveness work together as an elixir, this time soothing irritation and, in freeing you of it, freeing you to build something positive instead.

Remember this

Wherever there are people, there will be situations that call for understanding. Understanding allows forgiveness to function in all its holistically healing ways. Where we see the need, however we are able to forgive – be it, for instance, in acceptance, tolerance or conscious forgiving – let's do it, more and more.

Focus points

* In any confusing and/or difficult situation, seek simplicity, harmony and opportunity.
* Don't let the aggression you see in computer games and soap operas tempt you to follow suit. Forgiveness, understanding and a wish for reconciliation, peace and everyone's wellbeing are what real life is all about.
* If you or someone else has made a mistake and caused harm, see whether you can help put it right or in some way atone to make up for it.
* Be thoughtful and try to tune in to others and help them understand you, too.
* Break the cycle of bullying with firm boundaries and at the same time seek understanding, fairness and compassion.

Next step

In Chapter 8, Forgiveness and religion, we'll look at how forgiveness is a key tenet of all the main religions and how this essential wisdom can inspire us in our own lives.

Forgiveness and religion

In this chapter you will learn:

▶ *How forgiveness lies at the heart of all faiths*
▶ *What some of the major faiths say about forgiveness*
▶ *How religious teachings can enrich us, whether we have faith or not.*

It's a sad paradox that, while religion is often slated for being a cause of conflict, all the world's main religions have forgiveness at their heart.

Christianity is my spiritual heritage – the religion I was brought up to respect, if not necessarily to believe in, and whose tenets I generally accepted. But over the years I've been increasingly puzzled as to why Christianity and most other religions, too, get such a bad press. It isn't the fault of any of the major faiths in themselves.

Islam

The word *islam* comes from the Semitic word for 'peace' and, if we live in peace with others, we naturally follow a forgiving way of being. Islam teaches that God is the source of forgiveness and is named 'The All Forgiving'. When we've wronged someone, forgiveness may come from Allah or from the person, and the Qur'an states: 'Those who pardon and maintain righteousness are rewarded by God.'

Followers of Islam believe that it's better when possible to forgive someone rather than to be aggressive to them. It's understood that to be forgiven by Allah we need to recognize the wrong we've done and admit it before God, make a commitment not to do it again and ask for God's forgiveness. If we've wronged another person, we must, in addition, put it right and ask for their pardon, too.

The prophet Muhammad forgave others, even his enemies, for their ignorance and would ask Allah to forgive them.

Christianity

In the New Testament there are many examples of Jesus Christ's forgiving attitude and his wish that we should forgive others, too. The parable of the Prodigal Son shows us how important it is not just to forgive others in word but in actual practice by welcoming them back into our lives. He often said that those who are merciful will be shown mercy and that we should forgive and, if possible, seek reconciliation with those with whom we are in conflict. Over and over again, Jesus tells us to love our neighbours and our enemies and to do good, even to those who hate us, and to pray for those who mistreat us. He was clear, too, that we should not judge or condemn others, but that, if we forgave them, we too would be forgiven.

Remember this

Whatever our spiritual belief, the Christian Lord's Prayer is a lovely way to remember, each day, the need to be forgiving and to ask for forgiveness: 'Forgive us our trespasses as we forgive others who trespass against us.' It's a quick, clear reminder to continue or get back on to the forgiving way of life.

When Peter asked if he should forgive up to seven times, Jesus replied 'Up to seventy times seven' – that is, over and over and over again.

As Mohammed asked Allah to forgive others their ignorance, Jesus, on the cross, asked: 'Father, forgive them, for they know not what they do.'

While the Christian faith seems to believe that people are innately sinful, Jesus realized that we learn to do wrong as we grow up and live our lives, and suggested that we should not attack or punish others for their wrongdoing because we are prone to doing wrong ourselves. Whenever I'm feeling judgemental or bitter about someone or something, it always helps me restore a forgiving attitude if I remember what Jesus said when the crowd were baying for the punishment of the woman who'd committed adultery: 'Let him who is without sin cast the first stone.'

Judaism

Forgiveness is very important in this faith. If a person who has wronged us apologizes and tries to put things right, we should forgive them. In the case of murder, when only God can forgive them, we can forgive the grief they have caused.

Yom Kippur – the Day of Atonement – is the holiest day of the Jewish year when we apologize for the wrongs we've done and ask for forgiveness. It's also about taking responsibility for our actions, doing our best to make amends and beginning afresh.

Another tenet of forgiveness in Judaism is that, rather than stubbornly holding on to grievances, we should forgive and be easily appeased. 'When asked by an offender for forgiveness, one should forgive with a sincere mind and a willing spirit.'

The Bahá'í faith

The Bahá'í writings explain that we should love others for God's sake. If we do this, we will not become angry and impatient but will realize that humans are not perfect, and, remembering God, we will love them and be kind to them.

Complete mercy is advised and that, rather than focusing on others' faults, we should look at them with eyes of forgiveness.

Taoism

Taoism believes that we can live at peace with the world around us through the 'Three Jewels of the Tao' – compassion, moderation and humility – all aspects of a forgiving way of life.

The Tao of forgiveness is that we let go of our grievances against others and forgive them, freeing ourselves from the burden of bitterness and resentment.

Remember this

We should treat others with kindness and respect. It's also important to realize that, if we are not full of egotistical self-importance, we will not only invite attacks from others less often but, even where we do, we will be less quick to take offence and will continue to respect our attackers and respond to them positively.

Sikhism

In this faith forgiveness generated by compassion is the answer and antidote to anger. When we feel compassionate towards someone it dissolves any anger we may feel towards them, and so with compassion we invite peace, tranquility, humility and co-operation into our lives and our relationships with others. When we forgive it is considered a divine gift and not something of which we should be proud. God is kind and compassionate and forgives all beings.

Buddhism and Hinduism

In these faiths it is believed that everything we do comes back to us. Forgiveness is therefore very important to our personal wellbeing, as only in letting go of harmful thoughts towards others and thoughts of self and pride can we be at peace with ourselves, others and the world. As well as having a positive effect on our present, forgiveness and atonement are thought to have a beneficial influence on our future.

Loving kindness and goodwill to others may be contemplated in the practice of meditation, helping hugely in encouraging a forgiving way of being. Compassion and calmness are also reflected on and valued, all helping us to avoid and let go of resentment. Mindfulness is encouraged, too, and is part of the forgiving way of life leading to increasing wisdom and awareness.

Jainism

In Jainism forgiveness is cultivated as a virtue, both in terms of forgiving others and seeking and accepting others' forgiveness – not just from other human beings but from any other life forms that we have harmed. In prayer we may ask not just that we forgive and will be forgiven, but that we may have friendship with all beings and have no enemies. Confession and repentance are regularly practised, dispelling sins. By asking for forgiveness we have peace of mind, enabling us to be kind towards all living beings, pure of character and free of fear.

Ho'oponopono

This ancient Hawaiian faith is essentially the practice of reconciliation and forgiveness. In remedying or atoning for errors, their negative effects on ourselves, others and our environment are defused or erased.

Lessons for all of us

In all these faiths, forgiveness and a forgiving way of life – in general compassion, kindness and goodwill to others – are accepted as being not only of great importance but in fact crucial to our wellbeing and relationships with one another. To believers, they are also an integral part of their relationship with their faith and the creator and/or the fundamental energy and love of the world and the universe.

A sense of the sacred is at the heart of most religions, and it's something we can all feel and rejoice in. It reconnects us with the wonder of this amazing world and our good fortune in being a part of it and being able to appreciate it and each other. It helps us live forgivingly.

Prayer is another element of religion that all of us can practise and enjoy.

Religious or not, most of us do our best to behave well to our fellow human beings, other creatures and our world, but having a faith that reminds and urges us to do so can be a great help. Also, we're all too aware of our shortcomings and religion can be a wonderful help in encouraging us to forgive ourselves. In doing so, we get back in touch with our innate goodness and are enabled to keep trying to lead a good life, walking in the way of compassion and the whole spectrum of forgiveness. It enables joy. My sister put this into words beautifully:

> 'By the way, on the subject of forgiveness, I've recently come to realize that as God forgives me, so must I forgive myself. And that has allowed me to imagine myself being in God's presence without feeling I'm bad, but instead feeling joyful and happy. It's a big step forwards for me.'
>
> Dr Penny Stanway

How sad that there is sometimes enmity between and among faiths, and that terrible things are done in the name of various religions. This is clearly not the fault of the religions' essential beliefs but of humans' manipulation of words to serve their own malign purposes. They know what they do, but the religions would say 'forgive them' nevertheless.

It's only in forgiving those who cause harm that we can open the way to compassion, freedom from prejudice, and love and respect for others, whether or not we and they do or don't have mystical or religious beliefs.

Focus points

✱ Whatever your religion or spiritual beliefs, keep forgiveness and care for others as well as yourself at the heart of what you do.

✱ Forgiveness and making amends for the wrongs of the world gives balance, peace and freedom to move on positively.

✱ Pray and meditate; they are calming and help us connect with the energy of goodness that runs through humankind and our world.

✱ Connecting with the sacred sense open to all of us will remind you of your good fortune to be alive in this amazing world and the need to live forgivingly.

✱ Compassion, kindness and goodwill towards others are elements of peace and love and they feel good.

Rejection and forgiveness

In this chapter you will learn:

▶ *How we are likely to face rejection of one form or another in our lives and that forgiveness can help us overcome the painful feelings that it instils in us*

▶ *How to face rejection in a work or professional setting*

▶ *How to deal with rejection in personal relationships.*

How it hurts to be rejected! In the course of our lives it's probable that we'll be rejected by someone no longer wanting to be our friend/partner/colleague any longer. Perhaps something that we've made or done will be rejected or criticized. Most of us have been there at least a few times.

Case study: How Sheila advised her son

Personal rebuff or abandonment often happens first when we are children. Just this morning a colleague, Sheila, told me that her young son was upset because his 'best friend' no longer wanted to be friends. As well as feeling hurt, he was angry. This is a common reaction to rejection – despondency quickly transmogrifies into anger and, if not dealt with, it can become a thinly veiled resentment that seeps into the fabric of our lives, causing us to be over-defensive and spoiling new relationships. Fortunately, my colleague was able to help her son deal with the loss and his reaction. She empathized with him and gave him extra love and attention to comfort him. But most importantly of all, she helped him understand that people come and go throughout our lives and we, too, may sometimes be the one who moves on.

We don't set out to hurt each other, but sometimes we do. It doesn't mean that either of us is horrible. If there is insensitivity, that's usually down to embarrassment or emotional ignorance. If there is callousness, it's probably because someone has hurt them and they are copying that behaviour.

Sheila gave her son straightforward advice: 'Look, hon, it happens sometimes. Forgive him in your mind, shrug your shoulders, and be ready to make new friends. They'll come along – no worries.'

It was like a magic wand. As soon as he realized that he wasn't the only chap to be ditched by a friend, and was reassured that all would be well, he felt better. A feeling of being in good company helps a lot.

Tips for coping with rejection

▶ Tell someone you trust to be kind how you're feeling.
(a) Just admitting it lets a lot of the pain flow away. (b) It helps you get what's happened into perspective. If you see it's actually pretty trivial in the great scheme of things, you'll be over it soon enough. If it's huge, sharing it lessens the load.

(c) They may have some good advice; they will give you a hug; they will remind you that you're a lovely person.

- ▶ Remember that just about everyone has been rejected or has had something they have done or made rejected.

- ▶ Remember that, however miserable you feel about the rejection, if you let those feelings fade they will do so – quickly.

- ▶ Do something nice for yourself, just for you – a treat of some kind. It's a way of giving yourself a hug.

- ▶ Do something active like going for a brisk, long walk or going swimming. Exercise releases feel-good hormones that will take the edge off your sadness. The change of scene takes your mind off things, the pleasure of the pastime lifts your spirits and you realize that life is good – or soon will be again.

- ▶ Repeat my 94-year-old otherwise very proper aunt's favourite mantra: 'Don't let the bastards get you down.' And/or mine: 'Onwards and upwards.' Or Scarlett O'Hara's: 'Tomorrow is another day.' Or this one: 'Their loss.'

- ▶ While or after you've done all that, forgive the person who's hurt you. They had reasons, that you may or may not know; that's their story. Yours is to get on with your life, free of resentment.

- ▶ If you know their reasons and there are valuable lessons, learn them.

- ▶ If it was bad luck or unfair or you don't know why it happened, forgive the school of life. Press on, being your true self. Take an interest in others and be kind.

- ▶ If a rejection has left you feeling diminished or daunted, remember some good times when you've been successful and cherished. You are still that person. You are multi-talented (see my other Teach Yourself books *Simple Steps to Positive Living* and *Unlock Your Creativity*) and able. You can learn. You can develop your skills.

- ▶ Be compassionate to yourself and to those who've wronged you. If they were insensitive or even cruel, reflect that they either acted like that through ignorance or because they've been treated callously in the past.

Coping with rejection at work

There are many reasons why forgiveness is the perfect antidote to the hurt of a personal or work-related rejection.

Whether our work is rejected, we are sacked, made redundant or otherwise 'let go' by our employers, many emotions crowd in at the time and during the aftermath of the news. We may blame our employer or another colleague for doing the dirty on us or being mean. We may be outraged if we feel we've been doing a great job. We may, on the other hand, know or worry that we haven't, in which case we'll feel we've let ourselves down and be ashamed. Shame can also flood in if we're sure we've done our best; then we have to face the fact that perhaps 'our best' wasn't good enough. Shame may also be there if we realize we've behaved badly in some way, naturally enough prejudicing colleagues or our employer.

So our forgiveness may need to be four-fold: forgiving the colleague or employer who has hurt us; understanding the business set-up and dynamic that has made their action against us seem imperative to them; giving yourself tender loving care as you recover from the shock and/or indignity, and forgiving yourself if you know that you haven't done your best or have in some way behaved in a way you regret.

Even if you can't forgive your employer, you should try to understand that being in a management position is extremely demanding and that this may have put them under a huge amount of stress (to which sadly you fell victim). Understanding why they warned or fired you does ease the affront, as does having the generosity to feel compassion for them.

If your work has been rejected, continue to do what you do in the best way you can, putting anything you've learned into practice. Or if your usual work has dried up or isn't viable in the current circumstances or climate, be like the mice in the wonderful book by Spencer Johnson, *Who Moved My Cheese?* Don't waste time berating who's done you wrong; don't sit in a funk of despair. Set out with optimism and resolve to find another course of action, another destination.

Remember that liking people and liking their work are bound to some extent to be subjective and a matter of personal taste. So you'll never be able to please everyone, not everyone will like you and there will always be some who don't like your work. But many *will* like and love you, and many will appreciate your work – they are the ones who matter to you, just as you matter to them.

Remember this

It helps to reflect that employers, just like us, are imperfect. They are liable to get things wrong, misjudge people and situations, and not always be scrupulously fair. Besides that, they are probably under immense pressure to reach targets, cut budgets and above all produce a profit. Most loathe having to criticize or, even worse, fire a member of their team but they believe it is part of their job.

Forgiving when you're turned down romantically

Another kind of rejection often experienced is when a romantic approach isn't reciprocated. Years ago it was worse, perhaps, for women than it is today because it wasn't the 'done thing' for women to make the first move. They had to wait to be asked out or for a man, in the idiom of the times, to 'make a pass' at them. They could flirt of course, but they still had to wait, and if no invitation was forthcoming it could feel like a tacit rejection.

Today it's fine for women to make overtures and the huge popularity of Internet dating has removed any remaining stigma about women being proactive. The field has levelled and both women and men can make the first approach, so, although women don't have the potential hurt of fruitless waiting, we now risk our overtures being turned down just as men have always had to.

Case study: How Gee soothed his heartache

Gee seemed lacklustre but said that her day had gone well at work. I asked her how her new relationship was progressing, and she tearfully told me that it was all over: 'I thought he'd been acting strangely,' she said. 'He didn't return my texts as quickly as he had in the first few weeks and he looked shifty when explaining he had to go away for a few days on business, even though it took in a weekend. He didn't phone at all while he was away and only called me the next week when I asked in a text if something was wrong. He said he was finishing with me and there was no point talking about it as he wouldn't change his mind. A friend of his phoned me later to apologize for him, saying he'd behaved badly because he hadn't liked to tell me he'd gone back to his ex-girlfriend. I'm not only hurt now and missing him, but also angry with him for being so pathetic.'

We looked at how the confusion he'd put her through had made her feel undignified, and at how he'd mistakenly avoided confronting the truth of his feelings for fear of hurting her. She realized that she could restore her sense of dignity and inner strength by forgiving him for his clumsiness and immaturity. She felt a lot better when she understood his difficulty in being honest with her. I also pointed out that it's common to go out with several people before settling into a relationship where love is mutual and lasting. Sometimes we are the ones who bring a liaison to an end; sometimes we're the one who's 'dumped'. Next time we met she told me happily that she'd fully recovered: 'I realized why he'd been insensitive and that I'd actually been lucky finding out relatively early on that we weren't right for each other. Next morning I woke up and the pain had simply disappeared. It was as though in deciding to move on without blaming him any longer I'd simultaneously moved on.'

I've talked to many more men and women who've been keenly attracted to someone, only to find that the feeling is not mutual. Rejection may come immediately or may arise after a couple has been together for some time. Whenever it happens, and however gently it's put, it's likely to be hurtful and it's very easy to feel annoyed with the person who's hurt you and what often seems like the unfairness and unkindness of the situation generally – you were just being you; you didn't want to get hurt.

Most of the above tips for forgiving those who reject us socially apply in this situation, too. But there is additional advice that I've found specifically helpful to clients who have been rejected in a romantic relationship.

Attraction is a very personal and very subjective thing. Just think, someone you meet who is absolutely gorgeous looking, and/or the nicest, most interesting person on the planet, just might not do it for you. The spark is either there or it isn't, and has nothing to do with any kind of objective assessment. We can't help whom we fall for – we just do ... or don't. So the best thing to do is to feel compassion for the one who's inadvertently hurt us, for yourself, and for everyone who's ever had the same experience and, to adapt the words of the Frank Sinatra song, 'pick yourself up, dust yourself off and start all over again'.

Try it now: Start all over again

If you're not right for someone, they are not right for you, so let them go, wishing them all the love, luck and happiness in the world for their future. Be glad you met them, however short your acquaintance, and be glad that you have the freedom and opportunity ahead of you to meet someone where the spark and rapport is mutual. In the meantime you should enjoy the many benefits of being single. We're incredibly fortunate to live in a time and place where we can be equally happy and fulfilled single or in a relationship.

We look at forgiveness when a long-term relationship ends in Chapter 10, Forgiveness in relationships.

Remember this

When we undergo any kind of rejection, compassion, understanding, empathy, respect, actual forgiveness and love are all part of the forgiving spectrum, the forgiving way of life. Forgiveness takes away the pain of rejection and restores our equanimity and the autonomy to enjoy life. And, as ever, forgiving simply feels good.

Focus points

* It helps us get rejection into perspective and forgive the person if we remember that we are all likely to face rejection. It happens. Feel the hurt, then forgive and move on.
* If you were rejected unfairly or cruelly and can't just now forgive, resolve that you will be fair and as sensitive as possible when you need to turn others down.
* Should you realize that you brought the rejection on yourself, remember your ability and talents, give yourself a hug and aim to do your best in future.
* Remember that few managers like issuing warnings or firing someone. They are probably under massive pressure. An understanding of this helps tremendously.
* Romantic rejection can feel like the end of happiness. It isn't. Reminding yourself that you will recover all the more quickly if you are ready to forgive and move on helps you do just that.

Next step

In Chapter 10, Forgiveness in relationships, we'll focus on some of the relationships that are most likely to make an impact on our emotions and look at the valuable part forgiving attitudes play.

Forgiveness in relationships

In this chapter you will learn:

▶ *How forgiveness is a key ingredient in all relationships*

▶ *How the forgiving way can help us to understand and love our parents and our children better*

▶ *How, even at the end of a relationship, forgiveness can enable us to make sure that both we and our ex-partner can move on and flourish again*

▶ *How forgiveness can transform the workplace*

▶ *About forgiveness and friendship.*

Relationships give us the connection, interest, support and love that hold our lives together. We each have many kinds of relationship as we move through life. There are our families and our romantic partners and their families, our friends, colleagues and neighbours. We each have a relationship with our self, too. And, however fleeting, our contact with all the other people we meet or encounter is important as well. How we relate to people has a big impact on the way we feel, so our network of relationships is fundamental to our wellbeing. Our interaction with others fulfils, supports and sustains us, giving our lives meaning, purpose and happiness.

Forgiving our parents

Parents are our first love. We want them to be perfect – but of course no one is – and parenting is such a complex, often supremely difficult job – how on earth could anyone get it right all the time? So most of us have to adjust as we discover that our parents aren't perfect – and very possibly that they're very far from than that.

'They fuck you up, your mum and dad,' wrote Philip Larkin in his famous poem 'This Be the Verse', adding that they were messed up, too, and that it's a problem handed from generation to generation. This is a bleak outlook, but sadly one born of experience for some. Does it have to be so? Definitely not, as evidenced by the many who suffer pretty hopeless parenting and yet come through unscathed and very likely still loving their parents. The ability to survive parenting mistakes and even abuse and going on to lead a life unblighted by them is, I believe, down to forgiveness, with love or compassion at its core.

So yes, parents make mistakes – I doubt whether there are any that don't. Yes, they may damage us but fortunately the damage doesn't have to be lasting. Many of us weather the vagaries of our upbringing, forgiving our parents as we grow, and then, when we're adults, realizing that, while they may sometimes (or often) have got it wrong, they did their best, just as we will do when or if we have children.

'We do our best,' said my father to me when I'd rebelled about some aspect of his and my mum's parenting. 'Most parents do. You will when you have kids. We may not get always get it right but we do our best.' I've never forgotten it and I remember that, even as the stubborn, quite wild teenager I was then, I instantly forgave them and was flooded with understanding and love for them. I am again now as I remember them. They did make mistakes. So did I as a child – for of course children can get it wrong, too. (More on that in the next section.) The important thing is that we forgave and loved each other.

Key idea

Forgiveness in child–parent relationships is about trying to understand, giving each other leeway, keeping talking and even, in the worst-case scenario where you don't want to be with them again, staying in some kind of contact. Compassion is the element of forgiveness that's crucial to forgiving our parents.

The longing of small children to love their parents is innate and so is forgiveness – children have an extraordinary ability to keep loving, keep forgiving, no matter how little you'd think their parents deserve it.

Remember this

Understanding something of the difficulties our parents had through their lives and in their relationship to us helps us avoid the pattern of repeating their parenting mistakes as we bring up our own children. We don't have to pass hurts and damage down through the generations. We can all take a step back and resolve, not just to do our best, but to do it better than our parents and their parents before them.

But what happens when your parents are so hurtful that your natural love for them is damaged or in turmoil and forgiving them seems an unreal prospect or out of the question? There is always a way forward in compassion. I have witnessed over and over again how people's extremely negative or worryingly confused feelings about a parent can be totally transformed by the following exercise. Please don't do it on your own. Wait until you're with a good friend or a counsellor, as it can be very emotional:

Try it now: Forgive your parents

1 Decide which of your parents you want to forgive. If it's both, you can do the exercise focusing on the other parent another day. For now, I'll write as though it's your mum – if not, just change the 'she' and 'her' to 'he' and 'him'.

2 Think of your mum as she is now or when you last saw her.

3 Think of her when she was ten years younger than that. Picture her if you can.

4 Keep going back through her life in stages until you see her in your mind as she was when you were born. Imagine how she felt, holding you in her arms for the first time. Imagine the love she felt for you, her baby.

5 Now take yourself even further back in your imagination to her life before she had children. How was it for her, trying to make her life as an adult?

6 Then envisage her as a teenager. What was life like for her then in those transitional years? How did she feel about her parents?

7 Now go back to when she was a very small child. Innocent. Undamaged but so in need of love and protection. See her in your mind. Feel the love she wanted to give her parents and the love she longed and needed to receive from them. Hear her crying when they weren't always there for her.

8 Let your heart reach out to the small, so vulnerable child. Take her in your arms and hold her close.

9 That child you want, with all your being, to protect and who you wish and wish could have a life without difficulty and fear and with no feelings of hopelessness or abandonment, is your mum. Let the love and compassion you feel for her as a young child flow through you now, healing your feelings for her.

10 Feel your forgiveness washing away bitterness and blame, regret and resentment.

11 Hold the compassion close so that you can call it to mind again instantly whenever the old feelings of hurt resurface.

12 Give yourself a big hug, in your mind. If you're with someone, let them hug you and hold you close.

Forgiving our children

Forgiveness works its magic both ways – from us to our parents and from us to our children.

However good parents are, there is no guarantee that one of their children won't turn against them. Heartbreakingly, I've many times seen the pain of parents whose child has cut off contact with them. One client, 'P', said to me: 'My son "J" loathes me and I don't know why. I loved him and treated him just like his brother and sisters. They live near by and we see a lot of them. But "J" will have nothing to do with me. I swear I never did anything awful to him. Like all parents there were times when I'd get cross and tell the children off. But the others didn't turn against me. Why has he? I've pleaded with him to forgive me for whatever it is I've done to cause this. So has my wife. But he's turned away from us both.'

Sometimes, like 'P', a parent doesn't know what has triggered a rejection of their love. Sometimes they do know and it seems so insignificant they don't understand the child's extreme reaction or why the child won't forgive them.

But sadly, for all the thousands of good things a parent may do for a child, it can be one mistake, one harsh word, that the child remembers and holds against them. Or it may be one aspect of their parenting that might well have suited other children but which, unbeknown to the parents, was incompatible with this particular child's personality. Or perhaps there was a much more obvious harm that a parent cannot remember, has suppressed or is unwilling to admit.

Forgiveness is the healing balm that helps us to explore what's gone wrong and, where possible, to put things right, as much as we can. Counselling can be very helpful; family mediation, too. All or any of the forms of forgiveness mentioned throughout this book may help self-forgiveness and, in some way and over time, may help the child forgive.

It's not only parents who can get it wrong. Sometimes children make mistakes. There are no guidelines – or even, as far as I know, any self-help book! – on how to be a good child and treat our parents well. We learn as we go and hopefully respond to our parents positively and lovingly. But sometimes our children don't turn out the way we'd love them to be – adults who are pleasant and loving to us and get on really well with us. Sometimes they can be controlling and even hurt us. Perhaps they just don't like us. What then?

Keep your heart open and be ready to welcome your children back at any time they show signs of changing and wanting to know you again. Forgiveness means not harbouring resentment towards your adult children and not angrily questioning or judging them, not letting pride or hurt feelings bar the door to them. It means letting them try their wings and fly away – and come back when they're ready.

Key idea

Forgiving is being ready to make it up and to let love find its feet between you once again. Forgiveness is patience and thankfulness. Forgiveness is living in the present, not dwelling in the negativity of the past, and looking forward positively to the future, whatever it may bring.

Forgiveness between siblings

My mother-in-law, when she was five, carried her newborn sister down the path to the dustcart and tried to hand her to the men. 'We don't want her,' she said to them. 'Take her.' How I feel for that little girl, and for my own sister who also had to cope with negative feelings when I arrived. Fortunately, we made it through to become close friends, as the following personal story shows:

Case study: How my sister and I learned to cope with negative emotions and still get on well

'My sister was four when I arrived and, like all firstborn children who suddenly find they are no longer their parents' only child and that they no longer have their full attention, was flooded with negative emotions. She nonetheless coped well with these and was a wonderful big sister, helping me in countless ways, and was always a brave leader. But I was well aware how much I irritated her when I tagged along with her and her friends. And I wasn't the easiest of little sisters – I was quick to squabble with her and I know she could have done without that.

I could easily have resented her because she was often held up as an example to me by our parents and in many ways I rarely measured up. (I found out years later that in fact they had treated her in the same way.) We didn't have to forgive each other because we knew neither of us harboured malice for the other and much of the time we had great fun together. But we did have to forgive the situation we found ourselves in – being unwittingly pitted against each other by our parents. And unwittingly we ourselves played up to those roles, in a kind of competition we didn't want but found ourselves living out. Yet we did forgive the situation and our parents, becoming the best of friends and even closer as adults. My mother-in-law and her sister, too, became lifelong friends.'

The key in this kind of situation is to keep a forgiving attitude and be ready to like and love each other supportively, rather than being rivals. It doesn't always work out so well of course, and there's no rule that says we have to get on with blood relatives – after all, we didn't choose them as we do our friends. But we can all forgive the situation that sets us against our brothers and sisters and find it in our hearts to be compassionate to them. We can forgive ourselves for not always having been an angel (and no doubt being sometimes quite the opposite). And we can forgive them as well, because we don't know all that they went through as they grew up.

Forgiveness between a couple

When you fall for someone, become an item and maybe live together and marry, you are certain that the amazing love and rapport you share will last. But, usually, once the in-love phase that draws you together settles down and you see each other on a daily basis, you begin to notice each other's warts as well as their beauty. You might start to argue about things crossly, rather than enjoy discussing differences as you used to, and the other common relationship discords we looked at in Chapter 6 may start to crop up, too. This is a vitally important time in a relationship because you can keep all your relationship's loveliness, goodness and joy if you deal promptly and calmly with discord and remember to live forgivingly and to practise this for the rest of your time together.

Remember this: A checklist for a happy and comfortable relationship

* **Be kind, above all.** That means not making demeaning remarks, not being spitefully sarcastic, and not ever, ever, ever showing each other up in company. If you remember to be kind, you won't do these things – but *remembering* is key. The nicest people can find themselves being sharp, forgetting in the adrenaline of the moment that, if they cut their partner to the quick, their relationship will not only suffer but may start to bleed to death. It's a two-way deal, of course. So don't accept any less from your partner than kindness. You won't be doing them or yourself any favours if you do.

* **Don't let your tempers soar.** Usually my mother and father were very good to each other, encouraging, supportive and loving. That's not to say that they never disagreed or irritated each other – they did, often! But, if one of them lost their temper, their voice rising, a row brewing, chances were that the one taking the brunt would hold their hands up in a peacemaking gesture and say: 'Look. I'm your best friend. Let's work this out constructively, not shout.' Their willingness to stop themselves in their tracks and calm down probably saved their marriage – a good one despite their very different characters and strong personalities. They were forgiving of themselves, each other and their life (which was not an easy one in many ways) every day of their life together.

* **Veto the 'three Cs': criticism, complaint and control.** They are three of the most common contenders for reasons why couples are miserable or break up. If we criticize, moan about and try to control our partners, we make them and ourselves miserable. Constructive comment, positive encouragement and praise whenever possible, and agreed decisions and compromises lighten the heart and the weight of the problems of life alike. They nourish forgiveness. They sing the song of concord.

* **Crucially, watch out for a tendency to be controlling – both in you and your partner.** Ask yourselves: 'Do I have a right to control another adult's life?' Each of us, of course, is a free being and we should passionately defend our own and each other's independence and free spirit. It's all part of the forgiving way of life. So respect each other's autonomy. Instead of wasting time, energy and love in trying to coerce or even bludgeon them into doing what you want, work together, finding ways you can each be yourself while getting along just fine together, too.

Remember this

Love each other in all the aspects of your togetherness: as friends, lovers and partners and, if you have children, as parents. Each aspect of your relationship is a different kind of love – when all are appreciated and nurtured they make for a very rewarding relationship.

Forgiveness and infidelity

When a partner is unfaithful, even if the relationship has been rocky for a while, it's a horrible shock and possibly the deepest hurt we can experience or inflict. But it doesn't have to be the end and can even be catalytic in revolutionizing the partnership and revitalizing love. Forgiveness – or a forgiving way – is at the heart of recovery and healing and we'll look at this further in Chapter 11, Trust and forgiveness.

With the best will in the world, not all relationships are permanent. When one ends, forgiveness is vital in surviving the sadness and pain of breaking up and managing emotions and practical matters well without imposing more hurt and trauma. Can we really manage our emotions? Very much so. Where there's hurt we need to experience it, not pretend it doesn't exist, but there's a lot we can actively do to help ourselves recover. We need to remember that:

► the pain isn't permanent and that we will heal, get over the break-up and come back to happiness

► we have the ability to be aware of our emotions as they arise and actively stop them from making us behave cruelly to each other

► we can decide to be kind to each other. When asked how she and her husband Lenny managed to keep their separation and divorce amicable, Dawn French simply said that they were kind to each other.

We can be fair. It's easy, when you're hurt or frightened of being taken advantage of financially, to lash out at each other. Determine to be fair, both of you, and reach sensible agreement about who has what. Don't let friends, relatives or legal people encourage you to fight for more than what you are happy with or more than what is reasonable.

Forgiveness has a different view of 'more': more is good when it's more kindness, more understanding, more honesty, more generosity, more wanting the best possible compromise for you both. It's also more safeguarding of each other's interests, more remembering the love you have shared for many years with happiness, more being thankful that you had that wonderful experience together instead of sorrow that it's over. More solutions finding for the way forward. More agreement. More tenderness. More compassion.

It's never the complete fault of one person. It takes two to start a relationship, two to live in it together and two to bring it to an end. Forgive each other. Forgive yourselves.

Every step of the way through a separation we can look at it bleakly, casting blame, feeling bitter and resentful, feeling we've failed. Or we can remember the love we've had together and look forward to the happiness we will find independently again; and we can realize that it isn't about fault and failure but being ready to understand that the relationship has run its course and that we're doing the sensible, positive thing in separating as kindly and amicably as we can.

All this is part of forgiveness.

Remember this

Forgiveness sets you free from the misery of blame, shame and fear when a relationship is over. It feels good because it is healing and because it means you can go forward giving yourself the tender loving care you need. It feels good.

Forgiveness between in-laws

Our comedians never cease reminding us that relationships with in-laws are notorious for their tendency to be highly emotional and often volatile! But in real life it's not so amusing. When in-laws get up against each other it's usually because of jealousy, overprotectiveness and/or possessiveness. Let's look at how a forgiving way can help avoid or preclude the tension these cause and the conflict that results.

Jealousy of an in-law is all about fear – fear that they are better-looking, nicer, cleverer... Young wives and husbands are often in awe of their mother- or father-in-law. After all, they are more experienced, successful (or at least survivors of life), and have had years to add to their skills. They are probably more confident than you and most certainly know a lot more. Forgiveness means consciously appreciating this to pre-empt jealousy or envy, or acknowledging pangs of them and letting them go with a wry smile of recognition. You have all the time in the world to catch up, if you so wish, with their prowess.

Try it now: Create a forgiving relationship with your in-laws

1 In your mind, wish your in-law well and turn any niggling jealousy or resentment of their ability into admiration and liking.
2 Remembering that you can indeed decide to get on with them – do so and steer yourself towards actually liking them, too.
3 Everyone has good points – notice theirs and warm to them.
4 Remind yourself how much you love your partner, and how much they love their mother and father. You didn't choose your in-laws – you chose your partner so, for his or her sake, put yourself out to get on with them. Who knows? – you may find you come to love them, too.

It's much the same if you're a parent and find yourself jealous of your son or daughter's partner. The key to the forgiving way is to think of the love you have for your offspring and let that love extend to their loved one. It's about seeing their attractiveness and being glad about it. In other words, take jealousy by the hand and turn it round to liking, with love.

JEALOUSY

Jealousy of the love between your child and their partner, or your partner and their mother or father, can also be painful. You worry they don't love you as much. The forgiving way to deal with this is pragmatic. The love between partners and the love between parent and child are very different kinds of love, so much so that they can't be compared. Realizing this – and reminding yourself of it every time jealousy happens to rear its head – will help you let go of any jealous or envious feelings. So will, again, being glad that your partner loves his or her parents, or that your child loves his or her partner. You love your partner or your child, after all, so it's easy when you think about it to be glad that they have this other kind of love. Relax and welcome it.

Try to love your in-laws. Then, because it's hard to be antagonistic in the face of our in-laws' love for us, with luck you won't ever find yourself facing their dislike. But emotions being what they are, and not everyone being good at living the forgiving way and dissolving or controlling negative feelings, we may need to actually forgive our in-laws for some unfairness or unkindness or shrug it lightly off in a forgiving way.

Try it now: Overcome an in-law's unkindness

1 Understand that they are tortured by their jealousy – this will help you compassionately let it pass you by without retaliating or simmering with resentment.
2 Shrug your shoulders and let their unkindness drop off you.
3 Send a wave of compassion to them.
4 At all costs, don't blame your partner or child or take him or her to task about your in-law's behaviour. Remember that their loyalties are divided – don't make this impossible for them.

OVERPROTECTIVENESS

As a parent we naturally long to protect our children. It's a primeval instinct deepened by the many years it takes to raise them. So when you've reared your children, forgive yourself the ongoing urge to keep being proactively protective, particularly when you fear your son- or daughter-in-law may hurt them, and consciously back off. They can and will look after themselves. Hope and trust that they won't be hurt but know that you will be there for them if they are. That's all you can do. It's the forgiving way that will allow you to love and trust your in-law without being eternally suspicious.

POSSESSIVENESS

Once again, as with most emotions that have got out of hand or are intrinsically negative, this is based on fear. When we're possessive we're scared rigid that we stand to lose our partner's love or our child's to our in-law. It's a rational fear because it could actually happen. But chances are it won't because your partner (or child) loves you and wants that love to continue. Make it easy for the love between you to continue and thrive by not forcing them to divide their loyalty in your favour. As above, realizing that partner love is different from parent/child love makes it much easier to let go of possessiveness.

If you're a parent, the forgiving way is to recognize and accept that the time has come for your child to have a life of their own, including a partner whom they love very much. Be glad for them and wish them much happiness in their life together.

If you're in a relationship or marriage and feeling possessive of your partner and resentful of the love he or she has for their parent(s) and they for him or her, decide to be glad – really glad – for them. It won't threaten the love between the two of you. In fact, get them on board as your friends and allies and your mother- and father-in-law can help your marriage continue to blossom for years to come.

Above all, let go of the wish to be the most important person in your child's life, or if you're in a relationship or marriage, let go of the wish to be the only person in your partner's life.

Remember this

Realize that there are different kinds of love and that they don't threaten the one we have. Be kind, be welcoming, share your life happily with your in-laws. The more you treasure them, the more treasurable they will be.

Forgiveness in step relationships

One of the elements of the forgiving way, as mentioned in Chapter 2, is balance, and it's particularly important in relationships with our stepchildren. We and they are likely to experience the same sentiments and accompanying negative emotions as the ones so often involved in in-law issues – jealousy and possessiveness. But children's behaviour may be extreme as they live on their natural, spontaneous emotions. It's up to us, as adults, to maintain our equilibrium and not let our emotions swing into a state of negativity in the pressure of the moment.

Case study: How Laura coped with being a step-parent

Laura told me: 'Having stepchildren is very difficult. You have to constantly bear in mind what they've been through and how they're having to cope with a situation they would rather not be in. My stepsons openly wanted their father to themselves. They didn't want me around. But somehow we had to live together and the last thing I wanted was to be beastly to them and make matters worse. You can't be a pushover either, though, or they'll use it against you or take advantage. You have to stay balanced, not let it get to you if they say something unkind or are attention-seeking in a really difficult way. Above all, don't let them come between you and your partner. Apart from being tragic for you both if your relationship breaks up because of the stepchildren, it won't help them either. They need stability – that means that you and their parent are steady and fair and prepared to back each other up. And they need love. If you are consistently loving, balanced and fair, they will eventually respond – but I have to warn you, it takes time, so be prepared to forgive over and over and make Patience your middle name!'

It's easy to be objective about other people's fraught relationships with their stepchildren. We can see and empathize how difficult it is for the kids – they've lived through their parents' marriage ending, whether through separation or death, and now they are expected to live with a surrogate parent in the place of the one they're missing or grieving for. There are plenty of examples in classic fiction that tear our hearts for the plight of children dealing with a new parent and there are the 'wicked stepmothers' of fairy tales – the archetype being in 'Snow White' of course. But what isn't often portrayed is how difficult *children* can be – every bit as cruel and manipulative in some cases as the infamous step-parents! Children, however, can't rationalize or get things in perspective nearly as much as we adults can. So it's up to us to walk the forgiving way at all times, however hard it is (and I do appreciate how hard that can be!).

If you are an adult stepchild with bad memories of a step-parent when you were younger, perhaps Laura's experience will help you come to terms with what happened. For not everyone has the wisdom or fortitude or balance of Laura – some adults are just hopeless at being step-parents. I know that doesn't make it easier for you in taking away the injustice and sadness of the past, but it will, I hope, help you to, if not forgive them, at least let your anger and sadness be laid to rest. They were fallible. We all could be, if we'd walked in other shoes. Just realizing that is part of forgiveness. It can be a great relief and the beginning of healing.

Forgiveness can also be needed when, as an adult, a more elderly parent gets together with someone new. There may be worries, again, that the new partner will usurp the love between you and your mum or dad and take advantage of them or their money.

Case study: How Sam dealt with her father's remarriage

Sam, a woman of 50 whose mother had only recently died, told me she'd been appalled when her 75-year-old father fell in love and remarried. She found a forgiving way through her maelstrom of feelings: 'I was in a real state,' she said. 'I was upset that he was, I thought, being unfaithful to Mum; worried that the woman was in it for the money, and sad that I wouldn't be his chief love any more. But I could see how happy Dad was and that pulled me to my senses. I made a concerted effort to like his wife and found to my surprise that we got on. We've become friends and Dad's delighted. So it's turned out to be a win-win situation. I realize that I may lose what I can't help thinking of as my rightful inheritance if Dad dies before her. But life's too short to worry about 'what would happen if...' or about money. I tell myself, if I get anxious about it, that Dad's happiness is what's important – and that I like her. That's the truth, so there we go.'

Try it now: In a nutshell...

1 Don't fret about things you can't change.
2 Forgive loved ones if they have other loves in their life and don't have quite as much contact with you as before.
3 Be glad for the times you're with them or talk to them on the phone.
4 Celebrate their happiness.
5 Live your own life to the full.

Forgiveness and out-laws

I love the term 'out-laws', which one of my clients, Rose, gave to her ex-family of in-laws. She gets on famously with them and told me: 'Why wouldn't I? They like me and I them and over the years we've become close. We'd really miss each other – and miss out – if we cut off all contact, as so many people do when there's a divorce. Just because their relative and I got divorced doesn't mean we can't be friends, and neither of us want each other's families to disappear from our lives either. They're part of my life – a happy part – and we're all part of the same supportive network. They're my out-laws and I love them!'

This is a heart-warming example of the forgiving way in action – comfortable in the present and stretching into the future, too, wisely not looking back on the hurt involved in a split or any conflict that preceded it.

It's not achievable, at least not immediately, if your ex-partner and his relatives are adamant that they don't want to stay in contact. If this is so, you're best off forgiving them with all your generosity of spirit. Anger and resentment would hurt you more than them, so let them go, with love – or whatever degree of compassion you can muster.

Remember this

I know it's a cliché but it's very, very true that life is too short to bear a grudge.

Forgiveness between neighbours

One of the most frequent causes of stress is conflict with neighbours. It's liable to feel worse than disagreement with the other people we meet in everyday life because they are a physical presence in the area close to our homes, so we fear that they are a threat to us in our stronghold – our territory, our castle. Subconsciously, we can turn it into a siege or battle situation.

Try it now: How to defuse a dispute with neighbours

Before any disagreement escalates:

1 Turn on your antennae at the first sign that something might be brewing.

2 Stay calm.

3 Remember the wisdom of New Testament commandment 'Love your neighbour as yourself.' This doesn't mean you have to love him or her in the same way you love your best friends and family but rather in terms of being full of thoughtfulness and caring for them. You'll find that this has an extraordinary effect.

4 Reflect that they are a person just like you or your loved ones, with similar sensitivities. They, too, are fragile and imperfect – full of flaws even – but for all that likeable.

5 Whenever you meet or have dealings with them, say to yourself: 'This is a human being, vulnerable, probably afraid – that's why he's worried and/or hostile.'

6 See what you can do to reassure him that you are not out to hurt him.

7 Do not enter into an argument (see Chapter 6) or shout. If tempted, bite your lip. A moment's thought will remind you that it's not worth succumbing to the urge to lash back in temper or exasperation as it will only exacerbate the disagreement.

8 Be scrupulously honest and fair. Take the attitude: 'Let's see what we can do to sort this out and find a solution.' Solution-focused negotiation usually works. Of course, it may mean putting yourself out to, say, mend a fence or do whatever needs to be done to remove the annoyance. But it makes for a conflict-free life with neighbours, which is well worth the effort.

9 Arbitration may be helpful, too. Call on another neighbour both of you get on with and respect for a clear perspective of the situation, an opinion and advice.

If your neighbour can't see reason at all, there's still a chance that they might agree to a truce. If they are psychotic or so full of anger that discussion or negotiation is impossible, the forgiving way for your sake and your family's might be to call a truce or cease contact or – and I don't say this lightly – to move house. One couple told me: 'We tried and tried to keep the peace but our next-door neighbours continued to make our life a misery. It got so that we feared walking down our path. Not that they broke the law – they were too clever for that. In the end, we'd had enough – we didn't want to live alongside that kind of hostility – it was like being in a war zone. Much as we loved our house, our decision to move was the best one we've ever made. We have lovely neighbours now whom we're great friends with. It feels as if we've landed in heaven.' He added: 'We're very careful of our relationship with them – having had that bad experience with our last neighbours, we treasure our present ones.' That's forgiveness in action.

I should emphasize that bad neighbours are not the norm. In fact, it sometimes surprises (and pleases) me that the vast majority of us manage to get on just fine.

> ### Key idea
>
> Most conflict responds well to thoughtfulness and love – that is, respecting and honouring others while keeping our dignity. It's an important part of the forgiving way.

Forgiveness between colleagues

Work has yet another set of behaviours, and every working environment has its own nuances. Take time, in a new job, to settle into the culture, get to know the different personalities and see how the hierarchy works. It may well be that you will pretty soon settle into a place naturally, feel comfortable with the set-up and work well out of it. A relaxed attitude gives you the understanding that it will take a few weeks to adjust to the new work, environment and people and feel completely at home. During this initiation period you'll gradually get to know your colleagues, managers and employers.

If you've been in the same career and place of work for a long while, continuing or taking a forgiving, compassionate approach has the effect of making your office or other workplace a good place to be in. It's a lot about encouraging yourself and those you work with to be accepting or tolerant of each other's various foibles and not-so-good points.

However, although in a well-run organization no form of bullying or unfairness will be tolerated, realistically many places of work will not be so well moderated and it's always sensible to be alert to injustice or wrongs of any kind. It's easy to feel powerless about exerting a beneficial influence or bringing about positive changes, but don't underestimate your potential and ability to do so. The spectrum of forgiveness, including compassion, kindness and wisdom, actually gives us the potential to be hugely effective in bringing about good within a team and in an organization, just as it does in any realm of life.

Goodness and concern for others are always beneficial – and even when you find you're up against an overriding ethos or policy of no change, your stance and actions, if seeking the good of colleagues and of the company, will have a beneficial effect even if you don't immediately see it. It could, for example, sow the seed of better ways forward in working practices, or a kinder culture among the workforce that will blossom and come to fruition in the years to come.

Sometimes forgiveness isn't about turning the other cheek but, when your aggressor sees your wish to be friends as an annoying form of weakness, it involves being firm – not in a reciprocally malicious way but in a no-nonsense practical, positive way.

Sometimes, however well meaning you are to others, there may still be someone who seems determined to scupper your wish to be in accord with all.

Case study: How Emma managed a hostile colleague

Emma told me that she'd been dismayed to find that, despite her best efforts, one colleague had 'taken against her', seemingly doing all he could to make her life in the office uncomfortable. She decided to take a forgiving approach to the situation, ignoring the evident malice and trying to win the man, Ian, round with persistent considerateness and friendliness. But when she found out that he had been taking his unfair criticisms of her to their boss, she began to wonder what would be the best way to deal with his hostility, which was not only threatening her happiness at work but, now, also the job itself. A change of tactic was clearly needed.

Emma liked the idea of surrounding herself, in her mind, in a bubble that allowed her to interact with her colleagues as usual but formed an invisible shield against the man's veiled aggression towards her. When we next met I asked if she'd tried this technique. She looked lighter and pleased when she said, 'Yes, and it's had an extraordinary effect on my confidence. I'd been getting frightened of going into the office – it was like going into a battle zone, not only with his unpleasantness but with the way he was trying to turn everyone against me. But I only had to imagine being inside an invisible bubble of protection and I was able to relax and get on with my work, relating to the others in my usual unaffected way. I don't know whether it was my body language, but everyone seemed to relax, except Ian. I could see he wasn't sure how to proceed. Instead of making me nervous, as he had succeeded in doing before, I was now untouched by his bad vibes towards me.'

This could have been all it took to stop what was clearly a form of office abuse or bullying. But while Ian was careful now not to say or do anything against Emma around the others, he again tried to make trouble for her with their employer.

Emma decided to speak to her boss about it. He seemed uncomfortable with what he heard but asked Emma what she wanted him to do about it. She said that she had no wish to cause trouble and suggested that he tell Ian to back off and, provided he ceased being antagonistic, he, the boss, would not take the matter further. This unofficial warning worked. They to all intents and purposes got on from then onwards. 'I think he needed me to stand up to him,' Emma said. 'I didn't want to have to do that actively, but in a way it was probably a relief to him that I did.'

In this case, Emma was certain that she hadn't done anything to start or stir his resentment of her. But it's normally worth examining our behaviour and anything we have said for unintended or unconscious provocation. If you recognize something, this is a classic case where apology will almost certainly heal the rift and enable a good working relationship henceforward. Most people respond to the humility and regret that an honest 'I'm very sorry I said that (or did that)' represents. It's the powerful elixir of forgiveness.

Forgiveness between friends

Friendship is a living thing that thrives when there is mutual considerateness and, of course, liking and love. But the mix of these tends to be variable as the months and years go by, and forgiveness is a vital ingredient in the changing recipe of friendship that keeps it both fresh and comfortable. We all change and need to be flexible in the give and take of any friendship.

There will be times when a friend may not be there for you, for whatever reason, or you for them. Any change in the pace or content of our lives can bring this about, so that you find you're not seeing or talking to each other as much. Be forgiving about this. It's life and all we can do is accept it, try to stay at least in touch and be warm and enthusiastic about it when we are. Never close the door, as we saw above in the section on children and forgiveness, and don't hold a friend's absence from your life against them. One day the friendship as it once was may have the chance to resume – be ready to welcome it back, if so.

Friends may not always be loyal. Forgive them. We might say passionately we would die for our loved ones – but would we? Untested, we simply can't say how loyal we would be in certain circumstances or even in a thoughtless moment. All we can do is hope that, if we ever do let them down, they will understand and forgive us, and we will forgive ourselves for our weakness and strive to be stronger and more dependable in future.

There are many ways to be a good friend. Accept what is offered in a friendship without judgement. Love them for who they are, not necessarily for only what they do for you. In the same vein, do not measure your friends against each other. Love each one in his or her own right.

Like your friends. Liking is a lovely thing. It's a part of love, though many of us are embarrassed to say we love our friends. Let's recognize that we do, whether or not we voice it. Love is part of the forgiving way in friendship and acknowledging it, treasuring it, feels great.

Having said that, often love in friendship hums quietly along, sometimes active, sometimes not, but it's still precious, still an important part of our lives. There is strength in a liking that endures without demands.

Friendship and forgiving walk hand in hand.

Focus points

* Usually, getting on well with others is down to choosing to be comfortable around them and forgiving.
* We all make mistakes and we can all be annoying – living forgivingly is about compassion for our own and others' flaws and foibles.
* Kindness is key throughout relationships.
* Many problems are due to the intrinsic fear that lies behind jealousy and possessiveness. Understanding the reasons for the inner fear helps resolve the difficulties it creates.
* Solution-focused negotiation helps resolve most conflicts.

Next step

In Chapter 11, Trust, we'll look at ways we can encourage ourselves to trust others and them to trust us and the part forgiveness plays in this.

Trust and forgiveness

In this chapter you will learn:

- ► *That trust is a key part of forgiveness*
- ► *That you can make the decision to trust and be trusting.*

▶ How you can recover trust even after your trust has been betrayed.

Trust is integral to the spectrum of forgiveness. We need trust so that we are able to forgive in some way. When we doubt this, it can be helpful to put our trust in something larger than ourselves to help us – the strength and support of a religious faith, perhaps, or reflecting that to forgive, in whatever way we can, is part of the goodness of humanity and the only sensible way forward.

Trust, well placed, is positive, hopeful, faithful and immensely beneficial in two ways:

1 It allows us to live our life in the moment, happy and relaxed. The alternative is to live in cynicism and fear, suspicious, wary of the worst. Distrust does not feel good. Trust does.

2 It encourages that in which we put our trust to happen. When someone believes in us, it gives us a great boost of energy and that supplies the ongoing momentum to honour the trust placed in us. Trust walks hand in hand with praise and encouragement, enabling us to think: 'I *can* do this. I *do* have ability.' It's only one small step, then, to 'I *will* do this – I *am* trustworthy.'

Learning to trust is easier if we break it down into its elements. The first is choosing to trust.

Try it now: Decide to trust

1 Make a brave and positive choice to trust.
2 Be willing to change.
3 Walk in trust a step at a time, a day at a time.
4 Be glad each time you stop yourself fretting cynically and suspiciously.
5 Resist putting pressure on the other person. Your hope, faith and expectation are best sensed by them as undemanding encouragement and support.
6 Be joyful in the freedom from worry that trust provides.

Whenever the memory of betrayal or disappointment comes to mind, acknowledge its presence and then let it go. Re-forgive – and as many times as you need to. Remember that you want to trust, do trust and will continue to trust. Just as you walk the way of forgiveness, whatever form your forgiveness takes, you walk the way of trusting.

This doesn't mean being foolish. We need to be sensible, and trust is usually based on a logical decision that it's probably safe to trust. To trust someone, you ideally need to believe in their ability to behave right now in a way that merits the trust you're putting in them, their honesty about wanting and intending to do so, and their good intention towards you overall as well as in this particular regard. You also need to be confident about their reliability. Unless they inspire and uphold your trust in all of these regards, your trust will be threatened and perhaps shaken or destroyed.

But there is reason to have faith, even when it's not completely based on logic, because the knowledge that someone is prepared to trust us wholeheartedly is often enough to strengthen our resolve to behave well and our willpower to keep it up. A decision to be dependable for one day at a time is extremely helpful and comforting to anyone who wants to be trustworthy. Even if we have been chronically irresponsible in the past, with this day-by-day philosophy we are likely to succeed in living up to our wish of being trustworthy. It works for the person wanting to trust again, too.

Try it now: Trust someone today

Decide that today you will be trusting. Don't worry about the other person's ability to be honourable in the future – simply trust that, this day, they will.

Sometimes, though, there is no or little logical reason to trust someone or to re-trust them. They may be apparently feckless in their general life or have proved they can be so in their dealings with us. While it would be foolish to trust when that trust would put us in danger, when we intuit that they want to change, want to work with us instead of against us, trust – instead of logic – can be based on hope or conviction, a deep faith that they will live up to your trust.

Learning to be trustworthy

And it is something that can be learned. Being trustworthy is a habit, just as being forgiving is. With luck, we learn it as children. Our parents trust us to do all kinds of things, patiently teaching us what they want us to do and what they don't want us to do. They explain why and we develop reason. They put their faith in us and we love the feeling of being trusted and, in a sense, walking with our parents and other carers. It means we're part of the team and we flourish. As we are trusted, we learn to trust. But none of us is perfect, so sometimes we let the side down, and sometimes others let us down – our parents, even. By their example again, or other adults' and our peers', we learn that we can be forgiven, that we can forgive ourselves and that we can forgive others. And, simultaneously, we can trust again – ourselves and others, and they us.

Not everyone has this guidance, though, and we need to be aware of this, understanding and compassionate. This is all part of forgiveness. For being intrinsically untrustworthy may be natural if no one has bothered to teach you how to be trustworthy and how good it feels to behave honourably and dependably. This can be learned, thankfully, at any age.

Trust and safety

To keep trusting that a certain behaviour is happening or will still happen when clearly it isn't or won't would be foolhardy. There are times when we need simply to say 'no more' and call a halt to trust. Because you cease trusting someone doesn't mean you cease being trusting. On the contrary, you are trusting yourself deeply – to make the right decision and abide by it. You can still be forgiving even if you acknowledge that you can no longer put your trust in someone. If you can't completely forgive the person at this moment, you can forgive life. 'That's life!' 'These things happen' – catchphrases like these comfort us and remind us we are not alone. Relationships don't always work out and forgiving may be, and often is, about being flexible, accepting change and moving on.

Trust between couples

Most of us accept our culture's ethic of sexual and emotional fidelity in relationships. The promise to 'renounce all others' is the linchpin of commitment, even if we are not yet living together, in a civil partnership or married. We agree to and trust each other to be faithful. Or at least that's how we start out together. But many find trust very difficult for a variety of reasons.

For example, some of us are suspicious and distrusting even when our partner has done nothing to betray our trust. Forgiveness in these circumstances is a lifeline in letting go of fear and learning to trust. Suspicion that your partner is likely to be, or has been, unfaithful, when there is no history of such behaviour, is usually based on insecurity. Low self-esteem could be telling you that you're somehow unworthy of your partner's love and fidelity. A poor body image could mean you imagine he or she will be tempted by someone who is, in your belief, more attractive. Or perhaps you have previously been let down by a partner and fear it will happen again.

Self-esteem can be built and there are some excellent self-help books (see the Bibliography at the end of this book) and/or we can have counselling to help us discover the causes of insecurity and strengthen belief in ourselves. Most of us, even when we're usually confident, suffer at times from feelings of insecurity and suspicion. I've found that we need to remind ourselves often that we are loving and lovable and that our partner loves us uniquely and is perfectly capable of being faithful to us, just as we are to them.

Yet, in a strange way, facing the truth that there is no certainty of fidelity is extremely helpful, too. As human beings we are all fallible. But we're also astonishingly strong and resilient. We survive infidelity. You would, too, were your partner to be unfaithful; you would recover. But to live in fear of something that probably won't happen doesn't make sense. Facing our fears like this and thinking through them are immensely liberating and strengthening and enable trust to take the place of doubt.

Key idea

Trust is the panacea for all fear of infidelity. In a sense, you give your partner's free will your blessing in the hope, faith and trust that he or she will be faithful to you.

Remember this

Trust is powerful in encouraging fidelity and it feels good.

Trusting again after an affair

If a partner has betrayed our trust, we may feel as though we'll never trust them again. 'How could I trust him?' said Pippa when I first counselled her after John, her husband, had an affair. 'He's done it once – how can I ever know that he won't again?'

She can't know. But no one can ever know for sure that their partner won't be unfaithful. You could be unfaithful, too. Hard to believe? It's true. No one can tell, for sure, how they will withstand a temptation, particularly an all-consuming desire, until they experience it. We can hope and pray that we won't succumb, but there are a host of things including hormones, circumstances, feelings and chemistry, any or all of which could weaken our resolve.

Our potential fallibility doesn't mean, however, that any of us is untrustworthy. In fact, most of us are surprisingly faithful and trustworthy given the huge opportunity we have today to meet others, to give in to our feelings of attraction and to have affairs.

We trust that we won't. We trust that our partners won't. But even when our trust is betrayed, we can re-trust, if we wish, and forgiveness is the first key to this.

Case study: How Pippa learned to trust again

I suggested to Pippa that forgiveness and a positive way forward would be easier to contemplate once she understood why her husband had had an affair. Blaming and shaming him without knowing why he'd had an affair was destroying her respect for him. Confusion mixed with scorn fuels natural anger and makes it difficult to forgive. She agreed to look back at how they'd been together over the previous year or two, and to see whether she could fathom what he'd been searching for from someone else.

At our next meeting, she said: 'When I faced the situation, I realized that he isn't the weak man I was making him out to be. I've seen when other couples have been in this situation that affairs don't come out of the blue – they're a symptom of difficulty within the marriage. It's hard to see that your marriage is in trouble when you're in it, though. When I looked at ours clearly, I had to admit that our individual sex drives were mismatched. I'd been keeping John at arm's length physically, only considering making love when I spontaneously felt like it, which was increasingly seldom. And because I mostly didn't want to have sex, I'd stopped being affectionate, too, in case I led him on. Suddenly I realized how rejected he'd felt. No wonder he fell into the arms of someone who really wanted him.'

Pippa and John love each other and were keen to repair their marriage. Together, they negotiated a frequency of lovemaking that both would be happy with. 'I realized', Pippa said, 'that I could be enthusiastic about sex again provided John didn't keep trying to seduce me in between times. He is so pleased that I'm enthusiastic again he's happy with quality over quantity! A wonderful side effect is that we're really relaxed and affectionate again. It's like it used to be when we were first together.'

'And trust?' I asked.

'The minute I stopped blaming him for everything, I stopped distrusting him. He's not the sort of man who would have affairs for variety, and now that he feels loved and fancied by me he's content to be monogamous. The affair is history – our love is the present.'

Their mutual understanding, tenderness and positivity were forgiveness and love in action and all of these enabled a real, working kind of trust.

Knowledge and understanding of the reasons for a partner's infidelity help a lot and allow us to put things right where this is possible and when it's what both partners want.

This isn't the place to go into the many possible reasons why someone looks elsewhere for sex and/or intimacy. There are some excellent books on the subject, and seeing an experienced psychosexual therapist can be immensely illuminating and healing. Putting right what's gone wrong and/or what needs some attention and fine-tuning will help you to forgive and restore trust immensely. In a way, it's a mutual forgiving as you together restore your friendship and make decisions about whether you want to renew your commitment as a couple. Honesty is very important and surprisingly healing.

Key idea

Understanding makes compassion possible and means that you both take on responsibility for what's happened, for resolving what's wrong and for resuming the companionship, love and trust that once existed between you.

Remember this

Trust is precious – one of the most valuable gifts we give each other. Treat it as you treat each other – with reverence and with love.

Kindness, compassion, care

How much easier it is to get over mistakes, indiscretions and general fallibility if we continue to respect each other and be courteous, caring, compassionate – in general, that is, be kind. When we settle down together and commit to each other, we in a sense become kin. Kindness is a way of being – of treating others as we would like to be treated and as we treat our own kin. When we keep it at the centre of our relationship, it assures forgiveness in all its forms.

Focus points

* In general, be ready to make that leap of faith and be trusting. It increases the chance of a good outcome and it feels far better than distrust.

* Patience, hope and faith are all part of trust and the forgiving way.

* However trusting you are, continue to view the situation from all perspectives, remain astute and don't put yourself in danger when there are obvious warning signs.

* In a loving relationship you have to trust each other – it's like the oxygen for happiness.

* Forgiveness and trust go hand in hand. They feel good and they are your choice to make.

Next step

In Chapter 12, Disappointment and forgiveness, we'll look at the therapeutic nature of forgiveness in times of disappointment.

Disappointment and forgiveness

In this chapter you will learn:

▶ *How disappointments – past and present, forgotten and at the forefront of our minds – can poison our happiness*

▶ *How to uncover the hidden roots of disappointment*

▶ *How to take responsibility for your own life and not merely blame others or the 'way things are' for your disappointment.*

Any hurt or damage is disappointing and any disappointment is sure to cause hurt. But a forgiving attitude is a huge help as we recover and, depending on the degree of hurt, bounce back or climb out of the abyss.

Disappointment is part of the human condition. We can't always be lucky, successful and free from harm – we live in an incredibly complex world with fellow humans who are all different. Every single one of us is unique with an individual mix of emotions, abilities, willpower, wishes and every other human ingredient. We're bound to suffer disappointment and sometimes it's even self-inflicted, just to add to the possibility. As the Rolling Stones song goes, 'You can't always get what you want', and it helps us hugely throughout our lives if we accept this and bear disappointment as stoically as we can, shrugging our shoulders and moving on positively, forgivingly and constructively.

Key idea

How you cope with disappointment, whether others have disappointed you or you feel you've let yourself down, varies tremendously depending on your individual genes, the way you've been nurtured and taught, and your own experience. But, however you currently cope with disappointment, there's a lot you can do to learn not only how to better survive it but also to rise above the sea of resentment.

The main thing is to recognize disappointment as soon as possible when you feel it and get it quickly into perspective. This is the key to dealing with it and moving on forgivingly, without taking umbrage. We may not be able to assess it fully in the moment – that might take quite a bit of mulling over at a later date. But we can recognize the severity of our reaction and see immediately whether it's out of proportion.

Disappointments from a long time ago – and how to stop them continuing to trigger unhappiness in the present

We're funny creatures, we humans. Even when a relationship or situation that disappointed us happened years ago, we'll sometimes choose to replay it in our minds. It's like having an unhealed sore – you're subconsciously drawn to touch and fiddle with it, often exacerbating the original injury.

Do we actually choose to bring it up? Yes, we do. Certainly, we can't help having flashbacks, but where there is nothing constructive to be done about them we don't have to let them replay all the way through or even in part. By refusing to entertain the memory, whenever it resurfaces, we teach ourselves to let it lie at rest, at least most of the time.

Try it now: Let sleeping disappointments lie

1 Notice the minute an uncomfortable memory of disappointment comes up.
2 Say to yourself: 'Yes, I remember, but that's enough – I'm not going to think about it now; there's no point and it belongs in the past.'
3 At the same time, decide to forgive the past and move on.
4 Replace the memory with positive thoughts about other things.

It's different if there's unfinished business. Then we can bring all our positivity and practical sense to the fore to settle it. This might be difficult on your own or with the help of friends, however well meaning. A counsellor has the advantage of not being personally involved so they can stand back and help you to see the situation from an all-round perspective, enabling you to find your way through, so that, at last, you can walk away from it.

Compound disappointments

When we ignore disappointments, whether they are trivial or larger, or push them out of sight, they're liable to gather and become compounded. What happens then is that when we're disappointed in a similar way it triggers an emotional reaction perhaps much greater than the original one and possibly out of all proportion to what's just happened. We may feel there's much to forgive when in fact there's not really much at all.

In popular terms, we know this as 'emotional baggage' and it causes havoc in relationships of all kinds.

Remember this

Next time you respond with an excess of emotion to a small let-down, pay attention to the feeling immediately – this could help you stop yourself from overreacting and exacerbating the situation.

If you already have reacted – you might, for instance have left in a huff or got angry with the other person – paying attention will still help. The aim is to consider why you came to react so disproportionately. Of course, sometimes it's nothing to do with our past hurts. You may find, once you've looked at what happened clearly from both sides, that the other person was out of order and that your reaction was understandable. But if not and you realize that there has to be some other reason for the way you felt, then a little thought will probably be all it takes to track it down.

This simple practice is a catalyst for forgiveness. Revisiting old hurts enables us to forgive, depending on the incident, the perpetrator of the hurt or, if we know we were a part of it, ourselves. If it was traumatic and full forgiveness is not possible, we can still decide to let the past stay in the past and consciously move on from it, once and for all.

Case study: How Inge investigated past hurts

A client, Inge, realized that she kept taking offence when none was intended. Encouraged to look for possible reasons in her background, she realized that a few incidents in her childhood had made her feel vulnerable: 'I cried when I remembered these things that I'd buried. I was grieving not only for myself and the hurt I went through, but for the people who had no idea that their actions would affect me for so many years, causing me to lash out at anyone who innocently triggered the old feeling of hurt and fear.' We didn't meet again for a few months, and then Inge told me: 'It's changed my life. I'm not nearly so touchy. I bring a forgiving attitude into play whenever I feel ruffled, and try to live compassionately.'

Insights into past hurts – and the wonder of finally understanding ... and forgiving

It can be a revelation to realize that our behaviour now in reaction to a disappointment may be directly influenced and intensified by something that happened ages ago and has perhaps been totally forgotten. How many of us shoulder huge burdens of guilt that with true understanding can be washed away with forgiveness – whether of others, ourselves or both?

Love, understanding and forgiveness don't just alleviate old wounds festering with residual blame and shame: they cleanse them, enabling true healing from the inside out.

If something from way back is crying out for attention, understanding and forgiveness, it will come to you in time. It often 'arrives' first thing in the morning when we wake up, but it can come at any moment. Welcome it, even if you are busy and rushed and can't pay attention immediately. If it is welcomed, you'll remember it and will be able to pay attention to it later and think about what it means and how you feel about it.

Don't fret if nothing seems to come up that's interesting or helpful to your present situation and frame of mind. You've opened yourself up to awareness of things and feelings that you may have had in the past which are influencing the present. It could be that there isn't anything in particular and that's fine – forgiveness is needed only in the present.

Key idea

When you have a new understanding that affects your ability to forgive and accept forgiveness, it is a very real epiphany – an enlightening breakthrough that enables you, in forgiving others, yourself or simply the past, to live fully and happily in the present. It's a tremendous blessing. With love in your heart for yourself and for the world, welcome it, knowing it will let you forgive and live forgivingly.

When life is a let-down – and how a forgiving attitude helps

As kids we look forward to life with such zest and such high hopes. Yet more and more people suffer from disappointment-induced depression, finding they've little interest in life, work and hobbies and don't get much – or as much as they expected – from friendships and relationships.

It's easy to be disillusioned today because generally in the West we have unrealistic expectations. Advertising and the media constantly show us lifestyles we aspire to, but which in real life we don't always reach or even get a taste of.

So there's a lot of disappointment about, and that causes simmering resentment about the unfairness of life.

Case study: How Anthony turned his life around

'It wasn't supposed to be like this,' Anthony, 28, said to me. 'My parents had it so easy – they got a mortgage to buy their own house and paid it off. They kept their jobs and retired early with good pensions. It isn't like that any more. I've no chance of getting a permanent, secure job – my degree is pretty much worthless. And with the short-term contracts I have to accept, I can't save enough for a deposit for a house, let alone get a mortgage. I'm putting money into a private retirement plan, but it's unlikely I'll save a fund big enough to retire on with a decent income. It's not fair.'

I asked him to imagine how it would feel if he forgave his lot in life. He thought for a moment and then gave a big sigh. 'Actually, it would be brilliant,' he said. I suggested that he try doing just that every time he felt bitter, and that, instead of thinking about what he saw as his bad luck, he begin to have positive thoughts about his present life and what he could do for himself that would be positive. Next time we met his whole persona was brighter. 'I realized that I was wasting valuable time moaning about what I didn't have, and look out for other opportunities.' He'd enrolled in a new course, taken a few hours' local work to enable him to save, and started spending time on a new hobby that was good for him socially and didn't involve spending a fortune in bars and restaurants.

'I've turned my life round,' he said. 'Life may not be as easy as it might have been for the previous generation, but they had their problems, too. It's up to each one of us to find out what we can do, making the most of whatever opportunities there are, and do it enthusiastically. That forgiving thing', he added, 'is really helpful.'

'It's not fair.' I hear this protest over and over again, but interestingly it isn't just young adults who are disappointed with life but older people, too, the ones who have supposedly had it easy. So it isn't always about today's 'hard times', as Anthony suggested. The older generation may be disappointed by all sorts of other things, despite their pensions and the houses they've been privileged to afford. Environment issues are often cited as the cause of melancholy, as is boredom. We've become used to the idea that low-cost travel, food, entertainment and so on are our right and many are angrily disappointed that suddenly that 'right' is no longer always being fulfilled.

There's a way to fight this disappointment and stave off – or cure – depression, as Anthony found: through forgiveness.

Like most of us, as a child I railed against the hardship of not having something expensive that a peer of mine at school had. I knew it wasn't my parents' fault – they simply couldn't afford it, but still I said: 'It's not fair. Why should she have so much and be so lucky?' My dad said: 'You have so much too, if you stopped to appreciate it. And we make our own luck – you will have plenty of opportunities to live the life you want. Most of all, don't waste time envying others. Be glad for them instead of being jealous.' When I reminisced about this recently with a wise friend, Philip, who has decades of experience in the competitive world of design and events management, he agreed: 'Envy – gosh, how destructive that can be! It can eat away at you and poison your hopes and aspirations and it is totally negative. How much better it is when you stop grousing about others and love what you *do* have and *can* have.'

Try it now: Make your own 'recovery'

1 Instead of blaming the politicians who desperately try to keep the economy stable, adopt a forgiving attitude. That doesn't mean letting them off the hook, but accepting that they are human and doing their best, though they may not always get it right. People – politicians included – work best with encouragement.

2 Instead of whingeing (which feels horrible) constantly about those who have some control over environmental issues and blaming them for ruining this earth, stop ranting and take a keenly active interest, lobbying for environment-friendly decisions and practices in all areas of life.

3 Cease moaning about how difficult it is to find highly paid, secure jobs and blaming others and the time we live in, and accept, forgivingly, that those times are over, at least for now, and that we all need a different attitude to work. It isn't likely to be given to us on a plate. So be eager and prepared to work hard – if necessary, harder than preceding generations did, and very probably in different kind of work from what you trained for.

4 Become more flexible, willing to retrain and alert to and glad for opportunities to gain experience. Forgive the reasons why you need to be open to changing course, and view it instead as exciting and full of possibility.

5 Instead of wishing and hoping for celebrity and riches, forgive yourself for not 'making it' and forgive those who haven't spotted you and taken you to the top!

6 Love yourself for who you are and be the best you possibly can.

7 Instead of yearning for hip or luxury experiences, see the magic and goodness of life taken simply, enjoying the wonder that's there every day in everyday things.

8 Instead of resenting others who have more of whatever it is you would like, and letting envy and jealousy rack you with disappointment, be glad you have so many choices, so much freedom, so many good things.

Remember this

The life we have is rich in goodness. How lucky we are to be able to weather disappointments, forgive what we don't have and rejoice in the life and opportunities we do have.

Key idea

Choose a forgiving way of life. When you proactively give love, enthusiasm and energy to the world, depression fades, ousted by spirit and determination. You will have a great purpose. Enjoy being positive – it's powerfully good.

Focus points

* We all suffer disappointments and the more readily you shrug them off and move on positively, forgivingly and constructively, the less their negative impact will be.
* Don't let them build up – deal with each one. That way you won't store up emotional baggage that might adversely affect the future.
* Life isn't always fair but there are always happiness and wonder in this amazing world. So stay aware of all the goodness that abounds. It generously staves off the disappointments.
* When you're disappointed with others' behaviour (or your own), do something positive to encourage a better outcome.
* Love, enthusiasm and joy stave off disappointment therapeutically and extremely effectively.

Next step

In Chapter 13, Forgiveness and the power of stories and music, we'll look at how others' experiences of forgiveness light the way for us to lead a forgiving life, too.

Forgiveness and the power of stories and music

In this chapter you will learn:

▶ *That the experiences of those around us can provide invaluable lessons on the power of forgiveness*

▶ *That works of fiction and non-fiction – whether in books or films or on the TV – can help us to see a way through our hurts and disappointments*

▶ *That music and paintings, or indeed any work of art, have their own healing powers.*

We read to know we are not alone. We read – or listen to and watch dramas and documentaries – to see how others cope with life. We read for inspiration and support, and even the simple practice of reading can be very relaxing and help reduce stress. Other people's stories of forgiveness, whether in real life or fictional, can also be extraordinarily helpful in enabling us to think about our own situation and difficulties and can set us on the path to healing.

Key idea

Seeing how others have forgiven the perpetrators of their hurts and sadnesses is illuminating and encouraging. It gives us hope and the courage to go the way of forgiveness ourselves. And learning about the numerous ways there are of embracing a forgiving path opens a wonderful new realm of possibility, too.

Other people's stories

Opening up our hearts isn't always easy, particularly when something traumatic or sad has devastated us and we're harbouring anger of some kind or other. It may seem easier, in one way, to stay stuck in the grey area or sheer black misery of being unforgiving; it may even seem the *only* way. But then we read of someone who has been in the same state of mind as we are now. They were angry, desperate, seething with resentment, confused, appalled by the extent of someone's propensity for evil; perhaps all but destroyed by the horror of it all; perhaps depressed by chronic grief. And yet, almost unbelievably, we see that they came to forgive. It isn't unbelievable – it's what has happened over and over again in the past and can happen, now and in the future, for you.

Stories lead the way to forgiveness and show us a way to do it, not as a one-off act but in an opening up of your heart to forgiving. They show that, even if it isn't currently – or perhaps ever – possible to forgive the person who's hurt you, you can open up your heart to the myriad possibilities of a forgiving mindset.

The shining examples of people who've forgiven are legion. I list some personal favourites below, but you can find many more by asking friends for the ones that come to their mind, and also by asking in the local library or researching on the Internet stories of forgiveness in real life, fiction and film. Once you start looking for the inspiration of others, it keeps on coming.

In our own everyday life, too, we can see people who live in the forgiving way of goodwill to others. Look out for the people who:

▶ shrug off hurts and slights, making it up with colleagues, friends and neighbours

▶ channel their fear – and we all suffer from fear in all kinds of ways – into sympathy and support for others and do practical things to help ·

▶ are compassionate, realizing that everyone has their own personal cross to bear

▶ cannot forgive right now, but who channel recurring negative feelings like blame and rage into helping others rather than seeking revenge

▶ seek in countless practical ways to move on from hurt and pain, full of hope and plans for a better present and future

▶ refuse to dwell on and in the past but, learning from it as necessary, appreciate the wonderful gift of life and honour it with their positivity and engagement in the moment.

Case study: How Angela dealt with a traumatic experience

One such person is a friend of mine, Angela, who unbeknown to her happened to telephone while I was writing Chapter 16, Trauma and forgiveness, to tell me she'd been mugged in the middle of her home city. The thief attempted to snatch her handbag, knocking her and her friend to the ground in the process. A young couple rushed over and the man grabbed the thief, pulled him off and let him go.

Rather than opting for counselling, she preferred to talk to two or three close friends. As we talked, her thoughts unfolded: 'I felt violated. Being knocked over was a direct physical attack and no one has ever hurt me before – it was a huge shock. My bag contains such personal things – I should just have let it go but it was as though he was stealing a part of me. Afterwards other emotions kicked in, too. I felt irritable, snappy and fragile. When I looked in the mirror I didn't look like me – I looked much older and tense and frightened.

'It made me determined to digest what had happened and move on. Nobody can steal the inner me and I'm not going to let him steal my peace. I'll remember instead the kindness and courage of the couple who helped us, risking their lives, and the owners of the pub who took us all in and refused to take any money for the hot drinks they made us as we waited for the police. I'm going to have a weekend just for me – pampering myself, reading, eating lovely things and going for a long walk with my neighbour.

'I also have to count my blessings that we weren't physically damaged and he didn't get my bag so I don't have the hassle of changing locks, bank card, mobile phone and so on. I'm going to be sensible and buy a money belt so that I can keep personal valuables like these out of sight in future.'

She told me that she hopes that her assailant will learn the emotional impact of his actions: 'He just wants money. I wish he could learn how good thoughtfulness of others is and stop hurting them. I refuse to let anger and hate spoil my love of life and my inner peace – besides, what good would that do to anyone? What happened happened and I'm moving on.'

In her own pragmatic way, reinforced by her sense of her inner goodness, Angela realized that, if she became stuck in resentment, she would only continue the chain of blame, hate, fear and anger in which the man who had terrified her was himself caught up.

The magic of stories

There is something almost magical about stories and the examples of forgiveness they may contain. As well as inspiring and teaching us and leading the way, they leave us with a feeling of relief, of an energy flow of goodness and love, and an unexpected hope for a better, brighter future. I mention the film *Field of Dreams* below, and as I thought about this title the beauty of the song 'Fields of Gold' came to mind. Reading of, listening to and seeing examples of others' forgiveness takes us to a new place – a golden field of consciousness where redemption and resolution are not just possible but will happen when we seek it and want it to be a part of our lives.

The following have been shining stars for me along my own forgiving path:

▶ **Marian Partington, *If You Sit Very Still*** In this memoir, you share the author's pain and confusion as though you are with her in the years of wondering what happened to her sister Lucy who had disappeared, and then the years following the discovery of her body and the conviction of her murderers, the serial killers Rosemary and Fred West. But the memoir is hugely revealing of the complex and yet paradoxically simple ways in which forgiveness can come, and, over and over again, there are moments of such beauty that your feelings of horror are washed away with tears of joy at the ultimate forgivingness of her spirit.

▶ **Elizabeth Berg, *The Art of Mending*** This is the story of a family in turmoil because of the mother's abuse of one of the sisters when they were children and how, when it comes into the open after the death of their father, they struggle to find the courage to believe, find some understanding, and think about how they will move on as a family. Despite the turmoil, there is such a deep sense of peace and order refusing to be submerged as they seek some sort of resolution that you learn more and more about the nature of the forgiving way and realize, again, that forgiveness of a person as such is not always possible or necessary.

▶ **Anne Tyler, *Digging to America*** This novel explores everyday forgiveness in relationships within two families with strong connections. Again, this helped me immensely along the forgiving way of understanding and compassion.

▶ **My own novel, *A Piece of Sky Dancing*** This is about how three people come to terms with an affair and find their own way of resolution. It is based on a true story of people I'd known well, and as I wrote I was trying to work out how forgiveness and tolerance came to them. A love of beauty, life and peace plus love itself seemed to forge the alchemy of forgiveness.

Stories, then, are immensely powerful – they can open our hearts to life and to forgiveness. Not only do they teach and lead; they oil the creaky hinges as we practise opening our hearts. How we do that is individual and personal. It could be by doing something thoughtful for your local community, or a particular loved one, or your favourite charity. It could be in doing something positive for yourself. It could be in regenerating enthusiasm for your current work, or finding new work where you can be enthusiastic.

Forgiveness or a forgiving way frees and heals us, whether we've been stuck knowingly (resentful and bitter) or unknowingly (apathetic and depressed) in a state of unforgiveness.

Key idea

Other people's experiences show us how we can forgive, now or at some time in the future, and also help us tune into the compassion of the greater consciousness – the sense of others' compassion for all who have suffered and for all who have caused suffering.

They illustrate for us in glowing colours that every single moment of our lives we have a choice. To float or sink in glum or black thoughts, or to say: 'Just for this moment, I am going to have a positive thought.' It may not be something riveting or world-changing. It may be a simple prayer. And yes, you can wing out a prayer even if you're not religious!

We can also choose to meditate and below I have included a very simple mediation technique. Try it – it may seem impossible at first if you are full of anxiety and negative thoughts, but if you practise settling into the peace of meditation – even for a few minutes – you'll find that it becomes easier to undergo a shift of consciousness. Meditation is known to be even more deeply relaxing than sleep and, as a bonus, it's good for the heart and lungs, too. Most of all, it's good for realizing that peace is still possible, no matter what you've been through.

You can always access this respite whenever you decide to take a few minutes, or longer, out of life's cares and busyness. In learning that you can find peace this way and that peace, therefore, is there for you whenever you want it, you'll realize that there is a way other than the misery of anger and resentment or fear and shame. You can instead go the way of peace and forgiveness.

The power of music

Music can be equally cathartic in its own way. Listening to the music of a composer who has been to hell and back after suffering a tragic loss can especially help us be fully, deeply with our feelings and come back along a healing path. I'm thinking here of Eric Clapton's songs 'Tears in Heaven' and 'River of Tears'. The latter enabled my tears to flow after a loved one died after an accident. As I wept, I reached the heart and depth of my sorrow and afterwards felt extraordinarily peaceful. It was as though I'd been given the strength to start healing. Music can be like an angel that stays with you as you mourn and supports you as you work your way through your grief, however long that journey takes. The Adagio from Joaquín Rodrigo's *Concierto de Aranjuez* has the same deeply moving and cathartic energy, as do several of the great classical requiems. Paintings can sing to our souls, too, joining us in lament and helping us fly again.

Remember this

We all respond in differing ways to different art forms and examples of them. You will have your own choices – it's very personal and you will find the ones that sing to *your* spirit and help you in your personal journey through hurt. As you find them, recognize the feeling of meeting and being helped by a kindred spirit. It may feel like the literal meaning of the word – that you are getting to 'know again' the message that comes to you.

Your way forward is already there, just waiting for you to recognize it and follow it. The possibility of forgiveness is always with you. It is there to relieve you, to comfort you, to walk with you and to remind you to stay on the forgiving path – for it is your soul's right and your soul's salvation.

Focus points

* Other people's stories of forgiveness show us that it can be done and inspire us to think how we ourselves can forgive.
* As well as teaching us, others' experiences of forgiveness give us a taste of the relief and hope that it brings.
* Others' tragedies and trials give us a feeling of solidarity, strength and purpose – if they've been there, survived and forgiven, so can we.
* When forgiveness of a person is impossible, we see from others that there are other ways of forgiving and moving on.
* Whenever we relapse into blame, shame or bitterness, recalling stories of others' forgiveness inspires us to do the same and cheers us on.

Next step

In Chapter 14, Everyday forgiveness, we'll look at how a forgiving approach soothes the small but stressful annoyances of modern life.

Everyday forgiveness

In this chapter you will learn:

▶ *How sometimes keeping silent for a moment is better than the quick and biting quip*

▶ *How thinking for a moment about what we are going to say is more likely to get results than an angry, ill-considered rant*

▶ *How the little troubles of life are inclined to become overblown and how a little thought and care can bring them down to size.*

Staying out of the fray

In everyday life we have an immediate reaction to whatever happens and what's said, and we may be quick to leap in with our opinions, judgements and advice. People often say laughingly: 'I don't know what I think until I hear myself saying it.' That's OK to a certain extent. It can make for great conversation with an edge of excitement. But it can be dangerous. It's so easy to jump in thoughtlessly or carelessly and negatively influence the people you're with, yourself and perhaps the whole situation. One negative word, or even one meant positively but misplaced, can cause untold damage. Sometimes we're unconscious of what we're doing. All too often, though, we know how detrimental an effect our words may have, but we say them anyway.

We've probably been taught to exercise some tact and caution before we open our mouths. But this is soon forgotten when we get carried away, intoxicated by the sound of our thoughts and words, by the feeling of power we get and the way adrenaline flows and excites us when we're sounding off. Because of this high, it can become a habit and often we display what we think of as a laudable trait of outspokenness like a badge of honour.

It isn't. It's usually, contrary to our assumption that we're being clever and helpful, thoughtless and careless. It smacks of hubris when what's really needed is humility.

Case study: How Caroline learned how to break a bad habit

Caroline looked anxious as she thought back over her own tendency to be outspoken. 'I hate to think of the times I've waded into a situation or conversation, without thinking of the effect I'd have, or how helpful it would really be. So much of the time I've said things that haven't been helpful at all but have exacerbated a friend's anxiety and stirred things up. At least I know I do it now, but I can't seem to stop. And I want to stop! It's worse if I've had a bad day at work, or a row with my partner, or of course a drink or two. All these seem to increase my inability to shut up.'

'You can stop,' I said. 'We all can.'

We talked about some ways to check ourselves from making careless, crass and hurtful comments. 'Remember, and keep reminding yourself', I told her, 'to register it whenever you feel impelled to plunge into a conversation or take action. Ask yourself: "What's the way of peace here? Do I really need to contribute or would it be better to listen, or even sit together in silence? Will my words or my taking control honestly be helpful – or am I going to fan discord, worry or unrest?"'

Speaking again with Caroline a few weeks later, I saw that her face looked rested and carefree. 'It was really difficult at first,' she said, 'as so often I'm on the point of speaking too quickly with a negative effect – but I've been managing to bite my lip!'

'So what's it like now?' I asked.

'Now I find over and over again, when I pause before opening my mouth, that I want to say something healing. Or that I actually don't have anything very useful to say and that the world doesn't fall apart if I don't fill the silence. Nearly always, given my silence, the other person, having had a moment's respite to think, will say something else, thinking the situation through for herself. Or perhaps it's that the pause simply allows any negativity to disperse of its own accord...'

When we need to speak up

Sometimes, though, we have to speak out clearly, even if it means contradicting others. There is a valuable warning that we all need to heed: 'All it takes for evil to flourish is for good people to say nothing.' Yes, we need to speak out when something is clearly wrong, but there are usually ways of doing it constructively, which we're more likely to choose after a pause for reflection.

Most of us need to forgive ourselves for the countless times when our words or actions have increased others' anxiety or anger or for when we were afraid to stand up for goodness and right. In forgiving ourselves, we strengthen ourselves to resist the impulse to have a negative influence, and increase our courage to promote what's right. It's a decision we can each make. Peacemaking is part of a forgiving way of living. It starts with each of us. And it feels worlds, worlds better than promoting conflict.

Defusing negativity with a forgiving attitude

Case study: How 'J' learned to pause for thought

'J' told me she'd been irate that morning because she was disappointed with an Internet purchase. 'I wrote a caustic email and prepared to give harshly critical feedback on the website. Thankfully I decided to wait until I'd calmed down before I sent it. When I calmed down I realized the seller was probably unaware of the problem with the item. So I rewrote the email politely explaining what was wrong and soon received an apologetic reply offering to send a replacement. Instead of seeing them as the enemy, all of a sudden it felt as though I'd made a friend over the airwaves!'

A moment's thought about a forgiving approach had made all the difference both to 'J''s frame of mind and the outcome.

Try it now: Fostering positivity

Forgiving has many elements: when you are angry with someone for a mistake you assume they've made, be ready to do the following:

1 Forgive – or in a sense pre-forgive – by initially giving people the benefit of the doubt.
2 Be patient.
3 Be tolerant.
4 Accept that others aren't perfect any more than we are – we all make mistakes.
5 Be willing to learn more about the situation and why it's occurred.
6 Lead by example in being generously compassionate – it will encourage others to be helpful and understanding.
7 Be solution-focused – positively helping to seek a good outcome.

Many of the negative emotions we experience, such as jealousy and envy, fear, anger and rage, will diminish and often disappear when we look at them in perspective and with a willingness to examine the hidden reasons for our negativity.

The catalyst of forgiving ourselves when we can't forgive others

When we find it difficult or impossible to forgive someone for a crime or other grave hurt against us, or find any compassion at all in our hearts for them, taking a look at our own propensity for hurting others can be a powerful catalyst in breaking through the barrier of outrage and hate.

Try it now: Forgive yourself and your failings

1 Be aware of your own failings.
2 Remember that we are all on a learning curve as we go through life and don't always get it right.
3 Forgive yourself for your past mistakes and wrongdoing and resolve to try to avoid them in the future.

Our weakness and culpability are all part of the rich and complex story of forgiveness. Paradoxically, they can make us stronger, more compassionate and more determined to live better and support others in their efforts as well. All we need to do to work this alchemy is to remember and be ready to forgive ourselves – and others.

An attitude inclined to forgiveness enables us to forgive ourselves for bad behaviour and others for theirs and deal with the results of it constructively so that healing can take place.

Making it up to someone where possible by repairing damage done, atoning for it when it can't be mended, and showing readiness to move on in a better way without repeating the wrongdoing can, as we'll see in Chapter 20, Justice and forgiveness, help them to forgive and move on. Showing we understand the depth of the trouble or pain we've inflicted can ease the process, too.

More everyday forgiveness

In between the bigger issues of life we mosey along, living our normal, everyday lives peacefully enough. If only it weren't for the small annoyances that come up for most of us now and then. They have a tendency to flock together all too easily if we don't watch out, disturbing our general contentment and making us irascible and hard to live with.

It doesn't have to be like this. I once worked for a man whose day was a stream of questions and problems put to him to deal with. Did he get flustered or annoyed? Not once! He was a brilliant example and teacher of how to stay calm and tackle each issue thoughtfully and promptly. His forgiving gave all of us confidence and encouraged us to use our various specialties individually and as a team. It taught me a lot about how not to 'lose my rag' or equanimity. Here are the steps he used to deal positively with interruptions and other annoyances as they happened.

Try it now: How to keep your cool

1 Each time something comes up and you instantly feel irritated or worried, take a step back so that you can view it dispassionately.
2 Rationalize that the interruption is just that, an interruption, and that you can resume what you were doing as soon as this is dealt with.
3 Think to yourself: 'OK – I need to address this, that's all. What's to be done?'
4 Once you realize the first step, calmly, purposefully take it.
5 After that, work through any further actions needed logically and insightfully.
6 Each time you email someone or speak with them either in person or on the phone, assume that they will be helpful.
7 Speak at all times equably and pleasantly, not in a blaming or annoyed way.
8 Tell them what's happened clearly and slowly. If they prefer to talk you through what they need to know, answer their questions calmly, again taking your time if necessary. They can't help you until they understand the situation fully.

9   Assume that they will want to find a solution, as you do. Remember that most people, given the chance, want to help and to do their job well. Having a little confidence in them that they will and can do it, encouragement as they do it, and praise when they're getting there will all boost their determination to reach a satisfactory resolution.

10 Be gracious in all your dealings with them. This sounds obvious, but when we're worried we need to remind ourselves that they are much more likely to keep doing their best to help if you are nice to them.

11 Be gracious even if they don't succeed in resolving things. Losing your cool will only raise your blood pressure – and theirs.

12 Ask whether they can suggest your next step – for example whom to contact or who will be able to help.

13 Seek and retain a sense of perspective.

14 Give yourself tender loving care at regular intervals!

With the last two points it helps hugely to reflect: 'In the great scheme of things, is this such a big deal?' Usually, the answer is a resolute 'no'; of course it's not. When it is, however, a sense of perspective still helps, even in the worst of cases. Time and the hour, as the old adage goes, really do run through the roughest day. In a year or two's time, this, too, may be forgotten, or will at least be well in the past. You will look back and want to give yourself a hug, in your mind, for having to face what you're now coping with. Why not give yourself a hug right now? For comfort, for encouragement, for forgiving.

Sometimes when we get bogged down in frustration, petty or large, we feel we're going to be stuck there for ever. We're not. It's temporary. Just keep getting through it all, following all the steps – and you will get through as forgivingly as possible.

I had just written the last few paragraphs when my friend Chris called and we talked about it. She said: 'But, Jenny, sometimes we'd have to be superhuman not to boil over with annoyance or frustration. How about my way of dealing with it? I let off steam by going upstairs and punching a pillow as though I'm a boxer. Gosh, it makes me feel better. Then I can think about perspective and forgiving – not before!'

Good point. So when we can't just calm quietly down in the moment, here are some other ways to let that energy out safely:

Try it now: How to get rid of that pent-up frustration and aggression

* OK. Go punch a pillow!
* Go for a long walk. This could be on your own, with a friend you trust not to wind you up, or with a dog – dogs are the most forgiving creatures on earth and are so happy just to be out and about that it's infectious.
* Find some other oasis where you can breathe deeply and slowly, breathing out the tension as you do so.
* Meditate – rest in that oasis longer and listen to your inner wisdom.
* Take part in any kind of aerobic sport.
* Do some 'brain training' that you know you're good at – for instance a crossword or a Sudoku puzzle. As well as relaxing you, it will make you feel good.

Key idea

'Balance, balance, balance,' said Paul, a true carer not just in his work but in his life generally, 'that's what it's all about. Forgiveness helps us restore balance, whenever and however we've lost it. There is always another point of view, a back story we may never know. When we forgive or are compassionate in some way, or at least are willing to let go of bitterness and move on, we automatically move towards it.'

Darkness can never put out the candle of light, of hope, of goodness. When we balance our emotions, actions and words with a forgiving way, we shield the flame and hold it level so it can burn bright again.

Try it now: Be eager

'Eager' is a word not much used any more – but I'd like you to adopt it and hug it to yourself and your being. Be eager to forgive, eager to be forgiven, eager to live forgivingly. It takes the element of hard work out of forgiveness and makes it a good place to be, a good road to travel.

And being eager isn't only a helpmate to forgiving – it's the best of companions throughout life in all sorts of ways. And – like forgiveness – it feels brilliant.

Focus points

✳ Think before you speak and act and exercise tact and caution.

✳ Remembering your own weakness and culpability will help you to forgive others.

✳ Keep things in perspective. Ask yourself: 'Is this really such a big deal?' Usually it's not.

✳ If you need to let off steam, do it safely where you can't hurt others – punch a pillow, work out, go for a long walk.

✳ Always look for balance. Forgiveness helps restore it within and outside of you.

Next step

In Chapter 15, Overcoming resistance to forgiveness, we'll identify why we sometimes avoid forgiving, and how we can reduce this resistance.

Overcoming resistance to forgiveness

In this chapter you will learn:

▶ *About the hidden causes that prevent us taking up the opportunities provided by the forgiving way*

▶ *How our family heritage can prevent us from seeing the advantages of forgiveness*

▶ *How self-understanding and a willingness to face the truth about ourselves can help us towards forgiveness*

▶ *How the seeming advantages of non-forgiveness pale into insignificance when weighed against the advantages of forgiveness.*

The influence of our upbringing and background

'I'll never forgive them!' I've heard it said so many times, by so many different people in different situations. What they all have in common is the intensity and determination with which they say it. Often, they think they're getting their own back. And yet, as we've seen before, by not forgiving we hurt ourselves all the more, whereas if we forgive, in whatever way we can, it heals us and helps us move on and appreciate the gift of life again.

The tendency to be unforgiving often comes from others' example. No doubt about it, as we grow up our parents influence our attitude to forgiveness and our ability to forgive. They help guide and shape our innate personality, too (see Chapter 10). Unquestioned, their influence will last a lifetime, which is all very well if they were wise and warm, but not so good if it's made us, either generally or in certain ways, inflexible and unforgiving.

Key idea

The good news is that the more we understand about the nature of forgiveness and the release, relief and restoration of a forgiving approach, the more we can let go of our resistance to forgiving and manifest it in our lives.

Try it now: Break the cycle of negative influence

1 Think about when you were a baby. You'd have been quick to let your mother and father know that you needed something or that something was wrong. They'd understand and take care of you. Peace and comfort restored, all was soon well. No question of needing to forgive – you lived through the moments, loving and trusting and incapable of harbouring blame or resentment or worrying if you'd upset them. But soon you absorbed their attitudes and beliefs and to some extent copied the way they reacted to hurt, forgave and/or

accepted forgiveness. You'd have adapted, too, to the degree to which they led, or didn't lead, a forgiving life.

2 Now think of how this influence goes even further back, before you were born. For just as your mother and father influenced you, so their parents influenced them, and this goes right back through the centuries, each generation influencing the next.

3 As you remember your parents' ability to forgive and lead a forgiving way of life generally, realize that that is their story. They may never change. You can. You are free to make your own choices – free to decide to live forgivingly.

4 Feel the weight of the generations lift from your shoulders.

5 Feel the sense of freedom this gives. From now on, the forgiving way of life is your ethos, an inestimably important part of your life. You choose your own path and make your own choices.

6 Take the goodness of the past and its influence with you now, allowing it to keep helping you as you live well and kindly and open your heart to the possibility of forgiving.

7 Beware the advice of others who are bitter and can't forgive. It's hard to stay positive if you're with people whose habit is to moan, carp and generally be critical of others. And it's all too easy to sink into their negativity.

Key idea

So often this is actually what forgiveness is: a willingness to see a situation from the other person's perspective and, together if possible, seek viable solutions. That's balance, practicality and love, hand in hand.

Remember this

Weeping and anger are natural therapeutic reactions in the immediate aftermath of hurt. But the sooner you let homeostasis, your inbuilt healing mechanism, restore your balance as you think rationally and without a negative bias about how best to move on, the sooner you'll recover.

Case study: How Allie overcame the temptation to be unforgiving

'My best friend tells me not to forgive him,' said Allie when her partner had been unfaithful. 'She says he'll never be trustworthy and I'll wreck my life if I take him back. She says all men are weak and he's proved it. I don't know what to do. I love him, but she insists I'd be a fool to stay with him.'

While Allie's friend may have meant well, because of her clear difficulty with forgiveness and the general negativity that indicates an unforgiving prejudice against half the human race, she was hardly the best adviser. And yet Allie was wavering in the face of her gut feeling to forgive him and to give him and their relationship another chance. Negativity is like that and so is unforgiveness – they eat into your individual ability to be fair and constructive.

I didn't say that her friend was wrong or right. Just as each of us is unique, so is each relationship. Without counselling both of them, there was no way I could proffer an opinion or give specific advice – and even with the opportunity to learn more about the situation, their choices were still their own to make. But I did advise Allie to avoid the trap of soaking up her friend's negative attitude and to be wary of anyone who consistently uses words like 'should', 'never' and 'wreck' and who insists that all men (or all women) are weak or bad in some way. That's negative, prejudiced, pressuring talk. Instead, I recommended her to decide the best way forward positively, constructively and with compassion in her heart for both herself and her partner.

We looked at infidelity and other relationship problems in Chapter 10. But, as is the case with other hurts, forgiveness isn't about being a pushover or victim. It's about understanding, honesty and fairness and moving on sensibly and rationally.

After some thought, Allie and her partner talked and, peacefully and lovingly, managed to resolve what had been going wrong and move forward in unison. 'Just think,' she told me later, 'if I'd done what my friend told me to, we'd be divorced by now. It wasn't so much about forgiving him anyway; it was about working things out.'

The value of seeing the truth

I heard a philosopher on the radio say that the most important thing in life is seeing the truth. I think that's right, because if we didn't we wouldn't know what was real or what was false. To forgive, knowing our own truth and having as clear a perception of others' truths as possible, is crucial. Otherwise, we can become misaligned and misled.

Seeing the truth takes all our senses. You may see it with your eyes, listen for it, touch it and even catch the taste and scent of it. Most of us need to practise paying attention because in the busy-ness of modern life we tend to have a short attention span and all too often we do not notice what's going on around us. It's something that with practice we can easily improve. It greatly helps us to keep on the forgiving path.

The expression on someone's face as they or you are talking, for instance, their body language, the food and drink they prepare for you, the way they present themselves – seemingly little things like this will all give you clues to their truth at this time. Noticing and understanding it, even just a little, will awaken your inclination to be compassionate and let forgiveness – general forgiveness – flow through you. The more you see the truth, the less you can be taken in, so honesty becomes the norm between you.

Try it now: Use your 'sixth sense'

Perhaps the most important sense of all in 'seeing' the truth is our sixth sense. As you gather information with your first five senses, be aware of the atmosphere around them and between you. Perhaps it's mind-to-mind intuition or a kind of energy, like electricity, as yet to be pinned down by scientists, perhaps it's simply a coming together of all you're noticing with your other senses. Whatever it is, you will pick up on what it is 'telling' you more readily with practice.

Remember this

The more you're aware of others' wellbeing – or perhaps that they're troubled in some way – the more understanding and supportive you can be. Tensions ease, the atmosphere lifts and, even if only imperceptibly, you will make a difference. It's all part of forgiving – of giving something of yourself *for* them. It feels good, all round.

Are you in denial about your resistance to forgiveness?

How can you tell you're 'in denial' – that phrase beloved of psychotherapists?

The classic thing that rings warning bells that you are in denial about something is when it's suggested to you and you immediately deny it, probably passionately! For instance, if someone says 'You're angry, aren't you?' and you get really angry about it, shouting: 'No, I'm *not* angry. Of course I'm not – that's ridiculous!' it's a strong indication that you are.

Or someone might ask, 'Do you have a problem forgiving?' and you react indignantly by answering, 'Absolutely not – I'm a very forgiving person,' but feel extremely huffy. Whenever we deny a suggestion angrily, there's a strong chance we're in denial about the behaviour in question and are actually prone to it.

A counselling client, Zoë, who had relished discovering she'd been in denial about various things intermittently throughout her life, described it like this: 'It feels prickly, as though you're circling thoughts are crackly and crisp like cornflakes, only a lot more dangerous! I can recognize it instantly now if I'm climbing back on the old denial platform.' That's a delightfully graphic but highly personal description. You can have fun, if you discover yourself to be in denial about something, thinking how it feels to you. Like Zoë, remember that it's a useful tool in stopping denial in its tracks as soon as it starts to build at any time in the future.

Whether it's saying 'I've done nothing wrong,' implying that the other person has nothing to forgive us for, or saying 'Why should I forgive her?' or 'I can't forgive her,' I expect most of us have been in denial about the need for forgiveness at least from time to time. Usually, it's early after a serious hurt or conflict. We struggle to get our heads around the various issues that have been brought up, and in full defensive mode we deny we need to apologize or that it would show compassion and be beneficial for us to do some forgiving.

When we're in denial about forgiveness it helps hugely to have someone to help us think through the situation and its implications. I have two people I trust to tell me when my thinking is skewed and I'm being unfairly and misguidedly self-righteous and/or indignant. I know that, despite loving and rooting for me, they will look at the situation impartially and scrupulously fairly and tell me immediately if they think that I'm being over the top or out of order in any way.

It's often hard for friends to do this, though, as they may be not be used to standing back and taking account of both sides, and they may find it difficult not to side with you. So, unless you have someone who is both wise and capable of being impartial and honest with you, I recommend finding a professional, experienced psychotherapist or counsellor to help you review your defensive feelings and conflict-laden statements.

Sometimes we need to work out why we're in this state and how we can step out of it. But often it's quite simple – having held up a mirror to your attitude, you see it's time to stop being defensive and get back on the forgiving way.

Key idea

The forgiving way could mean letting go of your indignation and moving on with no more indignation or resentment, or it might mean saying sorry or accepting an apology. The point is to let go of any unnecessary emotional defensiveness and make peace – if not with the other party then at least within yourself.

Are there benefits for you in *not* forgiving?

You're eager to forgive and to lead a forgiving way of life, and that's great. Both will make a wonderful difference to your wellbeing. But continuing resistance to forgiveness may be strong, and for a number of reasons. Let's take a look at some of these, at what the benefits might be, and then weigh them against the benefits of being forgiving.

► Your conscious may be urging you not to forgive, telling you it would be stupid and insisting that you need to keep your defences up.

> ▷ *The benefit of non-forgiveness is:* you feel you're playing safe.

> ▷ *The benefit of forgiveness is:* free of feelings of blame and suspicion, you can move forwards confidently and happily.

► The unforgiving attitude of your parents and your family going way back exerts a strong pull on you to follow suit. If it could speak, it would say: 'This is the way our family does things. You can't escape it.'

> ▷ *The benefit of non-forgiveness is:* you feel comfortable staying within the traditional family attitude.

> ▷ *The benefit of forgiveness is:* you forge your own forgiving way of life which is right for you in the present.

► Fear tells you to always be on your guard, insisting that if you're soft people will take advantage.

> ▷ *The benefit of non-forgiveness is:* if you take no risks, you stay out of danger.

> ▷ *The benefit of forgiveness is:* you keep fear in perspective, using it the way it's meant to be used – as your ally in suggesting possible dangers but never as your jailer. You are thus free to be both sensible and courageous.

► Not forgiving is a habit it's hard to think of breaking.

> ▷ *The benefit of non-forgiveness is:* it's so easy to keep to a habit.

> ▷ *The benefit of forgiveness is:* with a simple decision and a little ongoing commitment you are back at the controls of your life.

► Not forgiving feels familiar.

> ▷ *The benefit of non-forgiveness is:* you don't have to think or change.

> ▷ *The benefit of forgiveness is:* in thinking and being prepared to change you step into a new, bright, warm, feel-good way of life.

It's a leap forward in self-understanding when we recognize we're stridently denying a truth about ourselves. Feelings can range from relief at having suddenly 'seen' it to an exciting realization of how good it feels to learn about our personal psychology and the way we relate to others.

It leads to more and more self-understanding as time goes by because, whenever you find yourself about to deny something, you'll pause to reflect on whether your denial is really justified or perhaps a construct to protect yourself and your image.

Forgiving requires us to be honest with ourselves in seeing the need and wisdom of it.

Remember this

When you break through denial and recognize how good it would be to forgive and to lead a forgiving way of life and be compassionate, you open the door to forgiveness, refilling you with your natural kindness and freeing you to let love be the guiding principle in your life.

Forgiveness in the face of lack of remorse

Over and over again, when I first talk with people about forgiveness, the question comes up: 'How can we forgive someone if they have caused untold harm and show no sign of remorse or apology?' This is a tough question. I put it to two wise people I respect a lot.

▶ The clinical psychologist said: 'We may not be able to forgive them as such, but we can remember that, given their genes, nurturing (or lack of it) and subsequent background, we might have become like them ourselves. We can be thankful that we aren't walking in their shoes now and find compassion for their unhappiness. And we can walk forwards in our own shoes, doing the best we can, living the forgiving way of life.'

▶ A lay reader and the very wise wife of a Church of England minister answered: 'Perhaps then it isn't our job, or within our ability, to forgive – so all we can do is hand it over to God.'

I think they are both right. If we open our hearts to the idea of renouncing outrage and hate, perhaps the pain will leave us of its own accord.

> 'I wondered if that was how forgiveness budded, not with the fanfare of epiphany, but with pain gathering its things, packing up, and slipping away unannounced in the middle of the night.'
>
> Khaled Hosseini, *The Kite Runner*

Life starts here. A new day. A new beginning. An epiphany with no need of fanfare.

Focus points

* Whenever you catch yourself saying something absolute like 'I'll never forgive him,' ask yourself if in fact perhaps you could and, if so, what's stopping you.
* If forgiveness isn't possible, you can still let go of hate, live forgivingly in other ways and move on.
* Learn about the background to crime and bad or delinquent behaviour – it helps our understanding, and collectively we can try to ensure that common patterns of behaviour are avoided in future.
* Welcome homeostasis – your natural healing ability – and help it along as much as you can.
* Take a look at the benefits to you of not forgiving. Compare them to those of forgiving.

Next step

In Chapter 16, Trauma and forgiveness, we'll look at the power of forgiveness to help you overcome what at first seems an unbearable event or shock.

Trauma and forgiveness

In this chapter you will learn:

▶ *That forgiveness does not necessarily entail forgiving the wrongdoer – it is about forgiving life and forgiving the world*

▶ *That we have vast untapped reserves of courage that can help us return to our lives, even though we will not forgive the terrible harm that has been perpetrated against us or an loved one*

▶ *That picking up the threads of your life is not an act of disloyalty but an honouring of yourself and your loved one.*

If you've suffered any trauma, it's advisable to see your doctor for advice. He or she may refer you to an experienced specialist who can help you.

Any event or shock that severely distresses us is traumatic and may lead to lasting emotional pain and anxiety. When trauma is caused by another person – for instance a terrible accident due to dangerous driving or a brutal physical or verbal attack – the shock is compounded and intensified by our reaction to the perpetrator. Hate, outrage and terror are all possible and very understandable. They may in time lessen, but it's likely that without help they will endure as seething resentment, anxiety and a desire for vengeance. Vivid flashbacks often bring all the horror back, fuelling our bitterness and inflicting the anxiety and pain over and over again. It seems to affect every atom of our body and mind. It feels as though we are never going to feel better.

It's difficult to write about this subject because I am very aware that for some people the advice I or anyone can give on surviving this kind of horrific trauma may be of no use whatsoever. Some who have suffered a cruel loss are unable to conceive of forgiveness of any kind or to take any step to climb out of their pain. To them – to *you*, if this is you – my heart reaches out. It's absolutely understandable – and although I myself have not experienced such a horrific trauma, I do understand. I hope you will nevertheless bear with me. Even if now my advice is of no use to you, perhaps something here will one day be of help. Perhaps you will be able to use it to help others through their darkest place of grief.

For those who are able to reach out, even if it's in the smallest ways, I hope that this chapter may prove helpful in your journey through survival and that hope and love will provide a light to light the way.

What forgiveness is and what it is not

First, it's important to be clear about what forgiveness *isn't* in the aftermath of a horrific trauma. It isn't necessarily about saying – and meaning – 'I forgive them.' It isn't condoning, in any way, the perpetrator or the crime or diminishing what they've done. It certainly isn't a panacea for what you're going through.

Forgiveness is, however, about finding something that will help you let go of the thoughts of ill-will and vengeance, terror and anxiety that besiege victims and often continue to overwhelm them, making any kind of recovery difficult or impossible.

Remember this

However hard it is to believe now, recovery in some form is possible, allowing you, one day, to appreciate life again.

It could be an idea, a chosen behaviour or a strategy that proves a catalyst for moving on from the horror. The hurt will never disappear – it can't, but it is possible to move forwards without it dragging you down, every day. It helps to think in terms of demonstrating your wish and determination to continue to live in accord with your own innate goodness and in goodwill towards yourself and others. That goodwill is not about how others behave. It is about *your* core, *your* being, *your* peace.

Key idea

You won't always feel this degree of devastation. Some degree of recovery *is* possible. Hold on to this thought like a lifeline.

Throughout this book we have been looking at the wide spectrum of forgiveness that includes the many ways that we can tread a forgiving path. In this chapter I hope there may be a catalyst for change that will help you let go of the besieging feelings and thoughts of ill-will to the perpetrators and those who ally themselves to, or defend, them.

Let's look now at ways that have helped some victims and their loved ones survive the first shock waves of trauma and the bleak desert of negative emotion that follows, and find their way through the darkness towards a happier future.

Keeping company and talking

In the black, searing hours of the greatest pain and grief, keeping the company of another, even when it seems that nothing ever will ease the pain, is helpful in at least giving you a feeling, as you talk or simply sit together, that they are sharing the overwhelming weight for the time you are together. It may seem a minute fragment of relief in the abyss, but even that fragment is good and helps survival. Most sufferers of trauma find that while talking with friends is invaluable, talking with a professional psychologist, therapist or counsellor who is sensitive to and experienced in helping victims of trauma is especially therapeutic. It's been shown that all the talking therapies are helpful when we're reeling from trauma. The help may take many forms:

▶ It allows us to share the burden of memories and emotions of the trauma, and it can be easier to open up about what happened with a sensitive, experienced therapist. You won't feel shy or embarrassed about discussing what happened and your feelings as you might with a loved one, and you won't feel you need to protect them from the worst of the details that haunt you. Again, with loved ones we can feel it's not fair to offload our burden on to them, whereas that is exactly what a professional is there for.

▶ It helps us understand, perhaps, not only what has happened (although we may never fully understand it) but, importantly, also how our feelings have been affected and how this in turn is affecting our spirit and our mental health.

▶ Cognitively, in time, we may be able to learn ways of developing our ability to cope with the effects of the trauma and begin to move on from it so that, in time, we can enjoy life again.

▶ We can explore, with the help of an experienced guide, the possibility of forgiving or finding other ways in the spectrum of forgiveness to help us lay down our negative feelings towards the perpetrator so that they no longer extinguish our happiness and peace.

Reaching inside yourself

When we find it impossible to understand the perpetrator of the trauma, and can only loathe and despise them for what they did, deepening our understanding of our own behaviour can help us find compassion for the tragedy of a world where human beings, with all their intelligence and potential for good, can become corrupt.

Again, this is not about forgiving *the perpetrator* or understanding *them,* but about taking time to look inside ourselves. We cannot stop anyone else – not even people we know well and our own children – from behaving wrongly, but we can look at our own behaviour, our own thoughts, our own impulses. We can recognize when *we* have had unkind thoughts, acted callously, let others down, let ourselves down. We can think how *we* can do better, be truer to the goodness of our nature, to our best potential.

You cannot heal or improve the one who wronged and hurt you, who inflicted the trauma that wrecked your happiness, but you can start healing yourself.

This positivity adds to the positivity of the world, not just your immediate world. It is part of the forgiving way.

Forgiveness, in any of its forms, is not sloppy and sentimental or some romantic dream. It starts with the thought that you will forgive or do something positive in the forgiving spectrum; it then becomes a decision and then continues as a concerted effort to move on from the horror of what's happened. In the devastation after trauma, you probably have precious little energy to think in these terms and make that decision or be positive in any way, let alone move on. But you can hold on to the fact that there is a form of forgiveness – doing something positive within the spectrum of forgiveness – that is possible.

Finding the courage

You have reserves of courage greater and deeper and stronger than you could have believed possible. No matter how weak and pathetic and wrecked you may feel, it is there at your core. No one, no thing, can destroy your soul and your inner strength.

Case study: How Joanne found courage after unimaginable trauma

Joanne, whose daughter was murdered after being sexually abused, told me: 'I felt as though I'd been reduced to a seething ball of hate for the killer, who was still at large, mixed with fear that he would come back for me. I thought I was a complete coward, and loathed myself for hating so much, too. But I read that visualizing ourselves as courageous can be powerful, and so with the help of a therapist I tried it. The guided visualization asked me to be in my mind the bravest person I could think of in a time of great fear. For a few minutes I became that person. It was as though I somehow drew down courage to me and the feeling of it flowing through me was tangible. It made me feel so much stronger. I took steps, with the help of the police, to protect myself.

'I used the energy of the previously all-consuming hate to resolve not to let him ruin my life for years and years or stop me from remembering and feeling the love between my daughter and me. Nothing can take that away from me, and I was – and am – incredibly fortunate to have that love and to have known her so well. Now that he's been sentenced, I've found that this new courage has enabled me to – not forgive him, I don't suppose I'll ever do that – but to feel sorrow for what must have been the hatefulness of his life and his soul to do something like that. I have the courage to go on and enjoy life as much as I can and not waste it on any more hate.'

Many victims who've gone on to walk a forgiving way, whether or not they've forgiven the perpetrator, mention the powerful effect of recognizing the underlying misery of the life that led the perpetrator to commit evil.

Picking up the threads of your life

Because someone has devastated your peace and happiness, it doesn't mean that these are lost for ever. Neither will negative feelings towards the perpetrator, like hate and fury, last for ever. Keep in sight that you – your character and soul – are essentially about decency, truth and goodwill to others. Do not be coerced into ongoing hate, bitterness, resentment and lust for vengeance. These are absolutely natural following trauma, but they do not have to hold you in their clutches. Remember who you are and know that you can, in the passage of time, pick up the threads of your being. This is not in any way about taking the moral high ground or otherwise feeling that you are 'better' than others. It's about being true to yourself and faithful to yourself, honouring yourself and your loved ones.

It may seem impossible to ever fully participate in or enjoy in any way your old hobbies, interests, other pastimes and work. But it is possible to revisit and resume them. At first, it may seem wrong that you are getting back into them. You may feel that you are in some sense being disloyal. In fact, it's the opposite – in doing so, you are honouring yourself or the person you have lost. In getting out and about again, you are helping yourself recover or at least get on with life and, in so doing, you will be better able to help others and in some way make this world a better place.

Even in the midst of bleakness, there is something we can do to restore balance – helping others in some way. You are not the only one who's suffered trauma. In helping others, your journey with them will help you as well as them. And for those who have not experienced trauma, but nevertheless don't have a completely easy ride through life – does anyone, truly? – you can be, through your practical help or by talking and listening to them, an inspiration and a guiding star.

Try it now: Help someone – now!

Think of something you can do to help someone right now. Notice how just thinking about doing a voluntary kindness lifts your spirits.

There will come times, unlikely as it may seem now, when you will find yourself enjoying life again. Perhaps, at first, it will happen only when you forget for brief moments what has happened. In these oases of freedom from pain, you may, for example, find yourself laughing about something, or getting fully involved in what you're doing, or truly interested in something that's happening to a friend. You are transported, for those moments, away from the all the horror. As above, please, please don't rebuke yourself when you recognize you are having a positive emotion. It's good. Hug yourself and say to yourself: 'That's fine. It isn't making light of the pain or being disloyal. It's the road of recovery and in healing I can better help others.'

Imagining forgiveness

Forgiving the perpetrator may seem an impossibility. Imagining what it would feel like is not saying that you will forgive, but could give you much-needed relief in the moment.

We saw in Chapter 3, Health and forgiveness, that forgiving has a very positive effect on our health. This is especially so following trauma, as any kind of forgiveness in the whole spectrum helps limit or reduce the significantly higher physiological effects of trauma such as raised blood pressure and heart rate and other negative effects of stress.

Remember this

Forgiving in any way also has a beneficial effect in helping us to bear and even lessen both the acute and chronic emotional pain we go through. I stress again that this doesn't necessarily mean forgiving as such and certainly not forgetting – it would be extremely unlikely that we could do either after a traumatic attack or accident.

Try it now: Imagine forgiveness

If you are used to meditating, follow your usual way into a meditative state. If not, sit comfortably with your back straight. Concentrate on your breathing; each breath, in and out, slow and sure. Drop any tension from every part of your body, easing in particular your shoulders, the back of your neck, your facial muscles.

1 Open your heart to imagining forgiving.
2 Remember that this has nothing to do with condoning the perpetrator or letting them off the hook in terms of justice. Remember that this is not for them. It is for *you*.
3 Say: 'I forgive them.'
4 Say: 'I free myself from blame, hate and resentment.'
5 Imagine that you are forgiving and have forgiven the perpetrator.
6 Imagine what it would feel like if you did forgive.
7 Feel the negative emotions of not forgiving falling away from you.
8 Feel the weightlessness of it. Feel the relief. Let it wash over you.
9 Realize that this feeling of freedom from unforgiveness, even though it is just imagined, is helping the process of homeostasis, your body's innate ability to refind balance and self-heal.
10 Know that you can do this at any time and feel the same sense of relief and healing.

The exercise of imagining forgiveness works because of the way any element of the forgiving spectrum:

▶ helps lighten the overwhelming burden of pain. It could, for instance, enable us to gain an insight into why the perpetrator came to act as they did, or to find a seed of compassion in our heart.

▶ gives a life-affirming positivity: even in the midst of horror, a moment of positivity somehow gives the psyche a surge of energy, helping you along the way to recovery.

▶ gives a feeling of recognition that *you* are in control of yourself. This is very enabling and healing.

▶ reminds you of your autonomy and your spirit working together.

▶ helps you regain a sense of balance.

Is it really possible to completely forgive a perpetrator when they seem to be wholly evil and show no remorse? It is certainly possible, but people who do so are generally regarded as saints or at least saint-like. For most of us, it would be an impossible and perhaps even unhelpful goal because we'd add the sense of being incapable of forgiving to our feelings.

But we don't have to let all the negative feelings take control of our lives for ever. We can feel the pity of it that a human being for whatever reason – genes, illness, poor upbringing, the effects of drugs and so on – has been transmogrified into a person who has been consumed by evil to such an extent that they are able to commit the most terrible deeds.

In feeling this sorrow and pity that this could have happened, you can strive not to let thoughts of ill-will in any form claw a presence inside you. In this way, sorrow is a kind of forgiving that helps keep your self, your soul, shining true.

Regaining control after trauma

This subject has been covered elsewhere in the book (see Chapter 7) but also has value here, in the survival of trauma. For when we've been traumatized, we are left feeling out of control of what happens to us. If something so monstrous can rob us of our peace, sense of security and wellbeing, how, we ask ourselves, can we ever feel in control of our lives again?

In a puzzling way, perhaps, recognizing that we *always* lack complete control, even when life is going smoothly and we appear to be in full control, is astonishingly liberating. Yes, things *can* go wrong – terrible things sometimes. We live in a world of great complexity and mystery and with fellow human beings who, though we all start out as innocents wanting nothing but to love and be loved, can be corrupted. And our planet itself can be wild and, sometimes, brutal. But then the realization comes: whatever happens we have our own inner goodness, our spirit, that intangible being that makes us our unique, authentic self.

And so, although others, in traumatizing you, have wreaked havoc in your life, turning your peace and fulfilment to horror and loss, they cannot take away your spirit, nor prevent you from taking up the controls of your life again. For while we can none of us prevent chaos completely, all the time, you can take steps to take back control of your life.

Case study: How Bea set out on the road to recovery

Angela, who (as we saw in Chapter 13) had been recently violently mugged, told me shortly afterwards how she was full of negative feelings but intended, that very weekend, to start taking steps to walk forwards, away from the sense of chaos and brutality. For her, it centred on giving herself tender loving care, as though she were physically ill.

'I'm going to pamper myself, lie in the bath first, then have some food – something simple and wholesome, then go to bed and read and listen to the radio. Then I'll get up and go for a long, long walk with a friend. And I'm going to plan a fitness campaign to get my body in great condition as a strong foundation for my mind.'

She added that talking over what had happened with me had made her feel a lot better. She could not contemplate forgiving the attacker, but knew that for her the practical steps she'd described would help her go forwards again in her old positivity, thus renewing it.

Try it now: Be good to yourself

Think about what you yourself can do that will feel relaxing, pleasurable and healing. It could be any of the things Bea chose, or something completely different. Sense how your mind and body feel better even as you consider the gift you're going to give yourself. Experiencing it will feel good, too. It may not take your mind completely off your grief or shock, but it will cushion you, and even the briefest respite will help your healing.

When we've been through a trauma it's totally understandable that the aftermath of emotion can so engulf us that we get stuck in it. It becomes a familiar way of life and even when new shoots of recovery and, in time, happiness come, it can seem somehow wrong and disloyal to be healing and beginning to enjoy life again. Perhaps, for those who cannot forgive or do not want to, it seems too much like forgiving. At such a moment all we can do is give ourselves permission to move on and let ourselves appreciate once more the precious gift of life we have. In honouring your spirit, you will honour your loved ones.

Focus points

✳ When we live forgivingly in any way we give a gift to ourselves and those around us. It also honours those we have lost. It is a part of love.

✳ No one has the power to control or diminish your spirit. In following a forgiving way, you take back control and grow in strength.

✳ Recovery is helped by a daily decision to think or do something positive.

✳ Remember – for it is precious beyond belief – that good is more powerful than evil and love is always better than hate.

✳ Welcome any positive thoughts and emotions that you find yourself having and encourage yourself to enjoy them.

Next step

In Chapter 17, Ways to help forgive and be forgiven, we look at ways in which we can help ourselves and others to forgive, live forgivingly and accept forgiveness gracefully.

Ways to help forgive and be forgiven

In this chapter you will learn:

- ▶ *How to avoid being judgemental*
- ▶ *How to apologize and accept an apology gracefully and constructively*
- ▶ *The difference between remorse and regret*
- ▶ *The difference between sympathy and empathy*
- ▶ *A simple relaxation exercise to use at a moment of strife or tension.*

Isn't it just so easy to lay down the law? However much more I learn and understand about living kindly, I still sometimes catch myself out feeling judgemental and harbouring suspicions or acting like judge and jury! I'm getting better at quickly checking myself and pausing to think, 'What am I doing? Where's my forgiving attitude and way of life?' That's all it takes, usually, to bring kindness or at least compassion back in and halt any harshness in my thinking.

Try it now: Banish judgementalism

Try doing the same – noticing the minute you start to be judgemental and replacing it with a total lack of judgement or at least, if your opinion is asked, absolute fairness. I think you'll be astonished not just at how good it feels to oust arrogant opinions and judgements but also how it beneficially affects the atmosphere around you and your connection with others, too.

People have always gossiped, of course, mulled things over and discussed the dramas going on in their circle. But now our thoughts and conversations take in stories way beyond the people we know. We have endless streams of human-interest stories ranging from gripping detective series to reality-TV shows and fly-on-the-wall documentaries – all encouraging us to decide and say what *we* think.

Certainly all this can help us understand what makes people tick, and having opinions is fine when it helps us be thoughtful. But when it simply stirs us up and encourages us to be arrogantly and pitilessly judgemental, it's a dangerous thing indeed.

Key idea

However tempting it is to jump in feet first and pronounce judgement of any kind, it's essential to remember to view the situation from everyone's perspective.

A good detective doesn't form an opinion until he or she has taken all the evidence and looked at the situation and circumstances from all possible sides. Juries are chosen to review all the information and discuss it for as long as it takes to arrive at a unanimous verdict. Only the judge – with many years of experience and, hopefully, great wisdom – has to make a decision on sentence.

> **Try it now: Stop being judge and jury**
>
> Try asking yourself, whenever you need to lose a judgemental attitude:
> * Why am I behaving as though I'm on a jury?
> * Who am I to judge another person when I'm a fallible being, too?

In all honesty

It helps us be forgiving if we are honest and truthful. Here are the definitions that seem to me to be relevant to the aim of living a forgiving life:

> *Honesty:* Integrity, truthfulness and straightforwardness

> *Truth:* In accordance with fact or reality

When talking with friends or counselees, I'll sometimes hear them accuse another person of lying or being devious. They find it very hard to forgive this. In a sense, their indignation is right – honesty and truth are two of the most important traits we have. However, it's a rare one of us who has never strayed from the path, isn't it? Haven't you?

Yes, we might try harder than some others to stay on the strait and narrow and yes, most of the time we may do so. But it's very, very easy to stray off it – and when we do, or have done, can we claim to be any better than others who have?

> **Try it now: How honest have you been?**
>
> 1 Look back over your life and, as honestly as you can, remember instances and times when you've been less than honest and truthful in any way.
> 2 Forgive yourself.
> 3 Decide to try to be more honest and truthful in future.
> 4 Forgive others who, like you, have slipped up.

It's important to know ourselves well in this regard because if we think we're perfect in honesty – that is, have never fibbed, or thought or acted unfairly, dishonestly or deviously in any way – it would be hard, if not impossible, to be compassionate. But as soon as you remember that you're not perfect and you have to work at being truthful and you're honest enough to recognize that you may stray again too, then it's much more likely that you'll be able to understand what it's like to feel someone else's difficulty and pain.

Key idea

When we acknowledge our own susceptibility to be less than truthful, we can cease being self-righteous, which is a pretty prickly, hostile way to be. It also enables us to forgive ourselves every bit as much as we're learning to forgive others.

The power of an apology

When someone says 'I'm sorry' – and means it – it's disarming. It's hard to stay cross or aggrieved when you're given a genuine apology. And it is a gift, and a generous one at that, because it takes guts to admit you were in the wrong. It feels good to apologize, too, once you get over the hurdle of deciding to and actually voicing it. It not only provides a welcome feeling of relief from the tension and a sense that you're doing the right thing; with any luck, it's also a way of dissolving or soothing the hurt you've caused and any resultant hostility, blame or shame.

Interestingly, if you're still at the defensive/aggressive stage ('Damned if *I'm* going to apologize!'), rehearsing it by saying the words 'I'm sorry' – either in your mind or aloud – can be all it takes to illuminate the situation, showing you that, yes, actually you do have something to apologize for. It's often reciprocal, too, because when we're faced with a generous apology it's as though a mirror is held up and sometimes you see that you too were wrong in some way. Often, therefore, if one party apologizes, the other immediately does so, too.

MAKING AN APOLOGY

▶ Think it through quietly on your own. Taking pride, fearful defensiveness and self-pity out of the equation, is an apology in order? If pride makes it seem difficult, imagine how the other person is feeling because of your actions. Remember that, if they are angry, it's because they are hurt, frightened and/or anxious about what's happened.

▶ If you realize that you've been in the wrong in some way, make the decision to apologize.

▶ It often helps, at this point, to write down what you did that hurt or offended the other person, and that you want to apologize for it. Writing it down (for your eyes only) will save you running round and round it in your mind. Tell yourself: 'What's done is done. I am going to apologize and with any luck that will go some way to making amends and putting things right.'

▶ Decide how best to make your apology. In person is usually best but if distance prevents this, then decide between a phone call or a handwritten letter. Beware of emails and text messages – they are easily misinterpreted and can be inflammatory, which is the last thing you want right now (see Chapter 5, Forgiveness and communication).

▶ In whatever way you apologize, remember not to be combative in any way. You are making peace: be calm, respectful and dignified.

▶ When you apologize, don't argue about their share of the blame (if they were partly to blame), or try to wriggle out of it in any way. Simply say you are sorry you did whatever it was.

▶ Say, too, that you are very sorry you hurt or, as appropriate, that you scared or made them anxious.

▶ If there is something practical you can do to put things right, suggest it and ask if you can do it.

▶ Try not to be too disappointed or upset if they are still angry and can't accept your apology at this point. Accept that this is the way they feel and take your leave of them politely.

- Don't let any negativity on their part make you angry or wish that you hadn't apologized. Remember that you have accepted responsibility for your behaviour and that your apology was and is honourable.

- If you feel very small and hate this, remember that showing humility is a sign of inner strength and compassion for yourself and others. When your apology is the right thing to do and a genuine expression of your remorse, it shows thoughtfulness, humility and kindness – and that you are on the forgiving way of life.

- If they seem to want to accept your apology but say 'How do I know it won't happen again?', state your full intention of not doing it again. Tell them what you've learned from the whole situation and that you have resolved not to let it happen again. If you are authentically determined to back up your apology with the resolve to improve your behaviour (or not let it slip again), then the genuineness of your intention will be clear. Look at them as you talk and speak softly but clearly.

- If they accept your apology but don't want to resume their relationship with you as before, respect their decision.

ACCEPTING AN APOLOGY
- When someone gives you an apology, accept it gracefully.

- Now do your best to leave behind thoughts about what has happened.

- If they have suggested a way to repair the damage done, extend your acceptance of their apology to agreeing to their making amends or in some way atoning for what they've done. If possible, make this as easy for them as possible.

- Don't take advantage of their wish and need to make it up to you. Be fair.

- Even if you are still indignant or angry, treat them with respect. Remember, it's probably taken a lot for them to get up the courage and resolve to say sorry.

Regret, contrition and remorse

You may ask how you are to know when an apology is genuine. There are no hard-and-fast rules for determining this – but we usually sense if an apology is truly meant. If so, it helps us to trust our intuition and the person if we understand the sometimes subtle, sometimes glaring differences between regret, contrition and remorse. The latter two are each the basis of a genuine apology, but regret may not be.

When someone shows remorse they have not only a deep feeling of sorrow at the hurt and damage they've caused but an accompanying sincere wish and resolve not to repeat them. Contrition is similar and usually involves shame and guilt as well, which all drive the person not to repeat the behaviour. Both remorse and contrition show a change of heart and the decision and determination to behave better from now on. It's a very personal choice.

Regret, on the other hand, is often far less personal. We can regret that we've hurt someone, for instance, but not be prepared to change our behaviour at all to avoid doing so again. Regret in some sense distances the apology from the person outwardly apologizing, so that in effect what they are saying is that what has happened is regrettable but that they do not carry any personal blame. This comes across as sneaky. Sadly, we're all too aware of politicians, CEOs and the like issuing such statements of regret, avoiding accepting blame in any way and refusing the notion of feeling ashamed.

When we want to help someone forgive us, regret is rarely enough. An apology founded on remorse or contrition is imperative; it shows an honourable emotional response and the prospect of healthy and healing change, altogether giving a very positive hope for the future and smoothing the path for forgiveness.

The healing power of empathy and sympathy

Empathy and sympathy both feel soothingly supportive to receive and they feel good to give, too. Though subtly different, they heal and can help forgiveness.

We empathize when we believe we understand what the person is feeling so that in a sense we share and therefore lighten the load. Sympathy is helpful, too, but is inevitably not as intimate or active a gesture since it implies you are merely feeling sorry for someone rather than understanding or even sharing their emotion, maybe because you have not experienced something similar.

Either way, we soak up empathy and sympathy like refreshing, healing water.

'Both are good,' said Cynthia, a counsellor. 'Sometimes you long to talk to someone who understands what you're going through; sometimes you just need a willing shoulder to rest on.'

I asked her to identify which of the two was best when and she said: 'Well, if, for instance, you've had a particular problem at work, there'll be times when you need to talk to a friend who you remember has gone through a similar situation. You know they'll understand implicitly much of what you're going through. No worrying situation is identical, of course, but you'll have a lot in common and in a sense share and therefore lighten the load of anxiety. It's just such a relief to talk to someone who empathizes. Understanding as they do, they'll also be happy to talk it over for ages, which is sometimes what you need. At other times that might perhaps be too intense a sharing process and then a sympathetic soul will be hugely helpful in their own right – they may be able to imagine something of what you're feeling, but basically they'll be happy to offer you a hand, metaphorically, to help steady you. They'll be there for you, even though they don't actually quite understand what you're going through, if at all, and that's a great help in itself.'

It goes without saying that both sympathy and empathy are only meaningful and helpful if they are genuine. Pretending to either is unhelpful and will only confuse the person because on some level they'll sense something is out of kilter.

Remember this

When heartfelt, sympathy and empathy are a much-blessed part of the forgiving way of life.

Relaxation

When a situation is fraught, recognize the emotional and physical tension and consciously relax as much as possible.

Remember this

Whether you are forgiving someone or being forgiven for something specific, or simply following a forgiving path by way of compassion, care and love for others, a forgiving attitude heals hurt and relaxes tensions. In the relaxation and restoration that forgiveness enables, you help others and yourself.

Enjoy the feeling of uplift and peace.

Try it now: A relaxation exercise at a moment of crisis

1 Centre yourself. Think of your solar plexus – the place in your midriff, just above your belly button and in the divide of your ribcage. Focus on it and feel it as the very centre of your being. As you do so, you will stand straighter, feel the ground beneath your feet, and be automatically strengthened and calmer.

2 Breathe steadily, a little slower than before, taking the breath deep into your lungs so that your diaphragm expands and goes down again with each breath. Whatever the ins and outs of the situation, remember that you want to – and are going to – take the forgiving way forward.

3 Sometimes a pause – a time of silence – helps calm the whole atmosphere.

4 Think love. By that, I mean think how you can lovingly decrease the tension in the room. It can help hugely to think how someone you know who is kind and wise would act lovingly. Or simply ask yourself: 'What's the loving thing to do in this situation?' Often just thinking about love has an effect on the whole atmosphere and eases any tension and hostility. It may be that others pick up on it intuitively or that your body language subtly changes, relaxing everyone.

5 Then, if you can, say something that will help make peace and/or make the other(s) feel better.

Focus points

✳ Watch out for when you start feeling judgemental. Decide not to judge or, if you need to, be scrupulously fair and, rather than blaming/shaming/punishing, think of constructive ways forward.

✳ When you know you're in the wrong, apologize promptly and generously.

✳ Accept apologies immediately and without reserve.

✳ Remember that contrition and remorse are more constructive than regret.

✳ Treasure the healing power of sympathy and empathy.

Next step

In Chapter 18, Forgiveness in loss and bereavement, we look specifically at the healing power of forgiveness in loss and sorrow.

Forgiveness in loss and bereavement

In this chapter you will learn:

▶ *About the complicated emotions that bereavement can throw up*

▶ *How we can forgive ourselves for not 'loving enough'*

▶ *How we can forgive God and the unfairness of life*

▶ *That negative emotions can recur and that forgiving never ends.*

The complicated emotions that may accompany bereavement

When someone we love very much dies, it helps so much if we keep forgiveness towards the front of our minds. For most of us harbour remorse and wish that one or other or both of us had behaved differently. As a friend whose husband died some time ago said: 'Bereavement is bad enough, what with the grief and the loss of a way of life. But then all these other emotions rear up and cosh you!'

Death is so final, so you'd think that grief would be finite, too, and that there'd be a normal time for it to last. Not a bit of it. Just as we are all different, so is every relationship – and everyone's experience of loss and grief when their loved one dies. When grief is complicated by regret, forgiveness enables understanding and frees us to mourn and also heal.

For many – perhaps most – of us, regrets gather in swirling clouds. They move around you, getting in between you and the light, always restless, demanding your attention. 'If only' becomes a mantra: 'If only I'd done this or said that' or, even worse, 'If only I/they hadn't done so and so or said such and such.'

Regret devours your peace and, unforgiven, leaves bitterness or guilt in its wake. So does anger. Anger in bereavement? Yes, anger is a common experience, too, and it can be overwhelming. How could they leave you? How could God or whatever force rules this world let it happen? How could life be so unjust?

These emotions, so strong and demanding, are part of the grieving process as we come to terms with our loss. We may naturally work through them until they calm down and fall into place as a natural part of the grief, and a forgiving attitude with lots of compassion for yourself helps hugely here. You may never stop missing them, but in time you find yourself remembering them with happiness and a smile of recognition.

Forgiving yourself and your loved one

Why are some people able to move on through the black feelings while others can't, or take far longer to? Though there are other reasons, the key to letting go of negative feelings is usually forgiveness.

Case study: How Les forgave his partner and himself

'The problem, though,' said Les, whose partner recently died, 'is that he can't forgive me, and he's not here so that I can forgive him either.'

We talked about his need to forgive himself for all the unsaid and spoken things that were haunting him and let forgiveness wash away the regret that he hadn't shown his love a thousand times more.

'If only', he added, 'I'd realized how much I love him before.'

'He would want you to forgive yourself,' I said. 'We are human. We make mistakes – sometimes hurtful, hurting, dreadful ones that we wish and wish and wish we hadn't made.'

I suggested that he express his remorse and let its healing power wash through him.

A few weeks later he said: 'It made a difference. I talked to him as though he were with me – said I was sorry, and I loved him so much. I know he forgives me and wants me to forgive myself. I still miss him, of course, but I feel so much better now. It's taught me a big lesson – if I'm lucky enough to love someone again, I will care for them dearly and show my love.'

As Les found, we can learn from loss how to love those around us more and to treat them better. We can learn to avoid repeating mistakes. It's a way of atoning for them and, like all atonement, it helps us forgive ourselves and move on.

Try it now: Give up guilt – accepting forgiveness in bereavement

1 Imagine how your loved one would comfort you if they could speak to you now.
2 Realize that they would not want you to beat yourself up with regrets. Feel their love and forgiveness.
3 And if this isn't possible because they weren't the forgiving kind, ask yourself: isn't it you who needs to forgive them?
4 Whichever way, let forgiveness heal and comfort you.

Running throughout the whole spectrum of forgiveness is the truth that comes up over and over again – none of is perfect. Not you or me or anyone. Our background, our genes, our character, our capacity for learning, our teachers and others we mix with, the way we develop and mature – all influence our behaviour.

However aware we are of our imperfections and try to behave better and love more, we aren't going to achieve perfection – and most of us of us know all too well that we fall far short.

Remember this

Whenever you feel regretful of your own behaviour to the one you've lost, or resentful about theirs, remember that you meant well and you tried. And you loved each other. Hold the love you shared close in your heart always. Know the truth – that they would forgive you and/or you can forgive them. Accept forgiveness, and forgive them.

Forgiving lets tears flow and dries them up. It binds our wounds and soothes the pain. Forgiving is the greatest healer of all.

Forgiving God or bad luck and letting go of rage

When we're fighting for a loved one's life to continue it can help to get angry with the seeming injustice of illness or accident and, if you're religious, God. Anger is natural and can help vent pent-up fear and grief then and after bereavement. But ongoing rage can sour you, turning into a bitterness that turns inwards on you.

There comes a time when we have two choices. We can abide in bitterness, or we can make peace with God or 'the injustice of life'. Doing so feels like taking a heavy yoke off our shoulders – in fact, that's exactly how Frank, a man I was counselling in his bereavement, described it to me.

We looked at the relationship between religions and forgiveness in Chapter 8, but Frank's story highlights how helpful religion can be in bereavement when we're angry about our loved one's death and lashing out at the seeming unfairness of it.

Forgiveness's part in coping with other kinds of loss

One of the losses we're likely to suffer at some point in our lives is theft of our money or other possessions, or damage to them. It tends to be painful far beyond the financial value involved because other considerations come into play. We feel victimized and vulnerable. This all leads to fear, anger and bitterness. Let this all fester and it can poison us emotionally and physically.

Key idea

Forgiving the perpetrator immediately is out of the question for most of us, but acceptance, hope for a good outcome and a positive coping structure, including preventative measures for the future, all help us keep our cool and maintain a healthy balance of calm.

I've talked to several people who have lost money through fraud and/or had belongings stolen or damaged but who refused to let it spoil their lives on an ongoing basis. Their observations on how they coped and moved on so positively can be summed up in the two points below:

1 They were buoyed up by the reality that there is relatively little criminal activity in our society. They believed deeply that the vast majority of people are not only trustworthy but do their best to put right anything that's gone wrong.

2 Money and possessions are important to us, of course. But they all came to realize that they are not what inner happiness and balance are all about. It's our own self-value, our work, our interests and, most of all, the people we like and love that make us.

Losing money or possessions only devastates us if we allow it. All these people made the decision that they were not going to allow the perpetrators to damage their spirit and enjoyment of life.

Remember this

This core belief in essential human goodness and our personal inner strength is something that we can all feel and nurture. It's very, very precious and it's there for us in all circumstances.

Let's remember again that in any loss 'All the darkness in the world cannot extinguish the light of a single candle.' Your spirit, truth and hope are inextinguishable and so is your ability to forgive.

Dealing with recurring negative emotions

Whatever form our forgiveness takes – from acceptance through tolerance to complete forgiveness – our initial feelings may recur. This is natural – our minds inevitably remember strong emotions and what caused them, whether we have willed it or not. I've heard people chastise themselves when they find themselves obsessing about regrets and guilt they thought they'd rationalized and genuinely forgiven. One woman said: 'I'd obviously not forgiven properly because here I am, going through all that blame and bitterness again.'

So let's remember this:

▶ There's no one way to forgive 'properly' – forgiveness has many forms, many ways, many different levels.

▶ We can't help painful memories and emotions recurring – they don't mean we didn't forgive.

▶ So we need to be ready to forgive or feel forgiven whenever those old thoughts and feelings pop up.

▶ Forgiveness is like love – we choose to love on an ongoing basis. Day by day, we behave lovingly because we want to and decide to. Forgiving is the same.

▶ We can dispel recurring negative emotions in many ways including through acceptance, compassion, tolerance, a sense of loving peace, and a conscious decision to move on unencumbered by bitterness and obsessive thoughts. In whatever way you can manage right now, forgive.

▶ Remember, it's for your wellbeing. A forgiving attitude or way of life will make a tremendous difference to you and your life.

▶ Forgiving keeps the channels open for goodwill, love and happiness in the present and future.

Focus points

* A forgiving attitude including lots of compassion for yourself helps hugely as you grieve.
* Negative emotions like guilt and anger can complicate the way we cope. The more we understand them, the easier it is to let them go and begin to heal.
* Have a conversation in your mind with God or an extremely wise person. It helps you sort through your feelings and imagine their supportive advice.
* Loss and bereavement are suffered by all of us. Keeping this in mind is comforting – we're not alone in our feelings.
* Even when we're feeling much better, feelings of grief are likely to recur. Feel them, let them go and keep living forgivingly.

Next step

In Chapter 19, Forgiveness and time, we look in more depth at the way time helps us forgive, live and move on.

Forgiveness
and time

In this chapter you will learn:

► *How time can be a great healer – to use that old cliché!*

► *How we can avoid becoming stuck in the past*

► *How we can learn to live in the present, enjoying pleasures both small and great*

► *How we do not need to forget to forgive.*

Time is intrinsically healing if we allow ourselves to heal. The healing may not ever be complete, and it doesn't depend on forgetting (see more on this later in the chapter), but if we are willing to forgive in some way and let the natural healing process do its work, hurt and pain ease and we can pick up the threads of our lives again.

How long does healing take? Time is a puzzling concept and often seems to have magical powers. In the blink of an eye our perceptions can change – or our hurt may take months or years to ease. Having a willingness to live forgivingly in some way is part of the healing process.

Living – and forgiving – in the moment

Over and over again we're seeing that forgiving is very much a choice we make. It's also striking that being a forgiving kind of person isn't one choice and one decision; it's a path to take each day and stay on, despite distractions that threaten to make us lose our patience and kindness.

Remember this

Every day we make many choices to live in a forgiving way. It feels good to be alert to this positive habit of forgiving and ready to pause and think so that we can encourage it.

Heightened negative emotion switches on a warning light, signalling the start of a cycle of blame or shame, defensiveness or aggression. Then you need to pay attention and figure out how to calm down, be rational and be thoughtful of those you're interacting with. How often? Do this whenever you're being judgemental or harsh on others or yourself. Living forgivingly is about living in kind: that is, the part of you – the deep heart of you – that is good and loving. We all need to practise it persistently because otherwise it's so easy to go off track and say things that don't help at all and actually make things worse – things we wish later we hadn't said.

This kind of forgiveness is about being mindful. When you're aware, you're present in this moment and in every moment. Even if you're naturally highly emotional and passionate, you're not at the mercy of your emotions; if you stay mindful of them, you can ride them like a wave – enjoying the good, positive ones, for sure, but noticing, too, those negative ones that can creep up on you or blast you out of the blue when you're least expecting them. If we're not present in these moments, things can all too quickly go awry.

Remember this

Mindful forgiveness gives you the chance to see the situation – and it takes only seconds – in an all-round perspective. It shows you a better way forward than the one where a hostile reaction would lead you.

Try it now: Be mindful

1 Pause.
2 Consider what's happening and where this is going.
3 What's an appropriate, fair and humane response?
4 What's the best way forward here – not just for you, but for the other(s)?
5 How can you manage this moment, this situation, with your thoughtfulness and good sense to the fore so that you all retain your dignity and have the chance to behave well and fairly?

It may seem like a lot to handle in the moment, but all it takes is for that pause to be mindful and everything will fall into place. Not that you will necessarily need to do anything at all right now. Often the best solution is to keep quiet, keep the peace and keep the faith that the best way forward will open before you when the time is right. One of the great benefits of mindfulness is that you won't get swept away by hostility, defensiveness, aggression or resentment. Unswayed by any of these you'll be free to be fair, lucid and balanced.

> Mindfulness = the forgiving way = balance, tempered with love and thoughtfulness

When the past keeps us in chains

Our brains are the most extraordinarily intricate mass of intelligences operating in the present to keep the body, mind and spirit working together in harmony. They have a great capacity to remember the past and they store not just what has happened throughout your life, but all the emotions you have experienced in yourself and observed in others. That's a massive amount of information which your brain is adept at sifting through so that when something happens today, it can pull forward into your attention anything that may be relevant. We need to ascertain quickly what is useful to us now. That rules out the vast bulk of the memories that would otherwise impede our efforts to live in the moment, confusing us and encouraging negativity. How can you get that focus? It's another learning and practising strategy – but one that's easy to do if you're keen to live brightly, alertly and forgivingly in the moment.

Try it now: Control your memory

1 Remind yourself that you are not at the mercy of your memory – its purpose is to help you live *today* and to enrich your life *today*.

2 So be firm. Ask yourself what memories and experiences you've had that you need to be aware of because they will help you now in a positive way.

3 Encourage them to come to mind by giving yourself some quiet time to think, meditate or just be.

4 Discourage and, if they still flood in, dismiss negative memories that are going to cause you to misconstrue what's happening in the present.

In this way you are equipped to deal with the present in the best way possible:

▶ You are in the moment – cogent, perceptive, thoughtful.

▶ You are able to use your experience positively.

- Your attitude to yourself and others will not be falsely coloured by inappropriate emotions.

- You stay open to forgiveness.

As we mature, we tend to become more tolerant and wiser and thus more understanding and forgiving. Those whom we hold a grudge against may also have changed and become more thoughtful or easier to get on with.

Key idea

It's hard to continue to harbour ill feeling when time has passed and one or both of you are no longer the same people you were when one of you offended the other.

When a forgiving attitude is our watchword, it gives us a good base for coping with everything that happens to us. On such a foundation of basic goodness, you can stand straight and stay centred. That puts you in the best possible position to enjoy life as much as you can and to deal with crises and hurts as and when they occur. You'll be less likely to be tempted to dwell on the sufferings of the past or to fear what the future will bring. You can concentrate on living now, doing the best you can, appreciating the goodness that is all around you.

Remember this

A readiness in the moment to think well of others or at least not blithely judge them when they disappoint or offend you is to move in the present and into the future as free as possible of shock waves, blame, shame, fear and bitterness.

Small things

Whatever has happened has happened. Don't let it spoil the whole of the rest of your life. Refuse to be in thrall to the past. It is not a prison holding you in among the bad times. You are free – you are living now and can use it as a valuable resource of experience and learning and a treasure trove of good memories. When you forgive the past, you set free the present.

Yes, we must grieve for our sorrows, repair, recoup and take the time it takes to heal. But we can retrieve our peace of mind even in the midst of this and know that we will, in time, rally all our reserves and enjoy life again.

Remember this

We can get through hurt. Often in cases of extreme hurt, that is what living in the moment means for us – staying present, living day by day, getting through whatever is darkening the light. And, even in the darkness, we can pay attention to our senses with love and thanks, as the moments go by, and use them again and again to enjoy the gift of life in this extraordinary world, whatever is going on in our personal life or humankind's.

Case study: How a grieving friend found solace in 'little things'

A friend was devastated by the death of her husband, who was and remains the love of her life. I asked her how she got through the grief and regained, in time, the customary happiness that seems to shine out from her. She told me: 'I owe it to the small things of life – the little pleasures and peaks that come even in deep depression if we watch out for them. It doesn't lift you out of the trough of despair, but it helps you forgive the meanness of life we're all going to face at times. It helps you hang on in there, believing that one day you will climb out and life will be good again.'

'The small things?'

'Very small, most people would probably call them. They'd perhaps scoff at me and call it – and me, come to that – trivial. But there it is, they help me and give me pleasure, all the time. Like having boiled eggs and wholemeal toast for supper. Comfort food, of course – but delicious, nourishing, beautiful. Or sitting somewhere warm with the cat on my lap. Looking at a new moon one night, surrounded by a pale pink, glowing aura. Seeing the first smiles of my daughter's baby. Her (my daughter's) kindness to me and my friends' support. Things like these are there for us every day if you look out for them – they are what helped me through.'

'It's about love, in a way, isn't it?' I asked.

'Yes, now I think about it. I kept my self-respect and looked after myself – that's a kind of love. The cat, the moon, my daughter, her baby, friendship – all these are love, aren't they?'

'Maybe the little things aren't so little.'

She smiled and said: 'They're pretty massive.'

Whatever's happening in our lives, we can see and hold fast to the beauty of love. There is the kindness of friends and strangers and our own kindness to others. Then there are the small everyday pleasures: even when they are wrested from us by events – for instance in wartime – no one can take away our memories of them. No one can destroy our spirit, either.

Remember this

We can always connect with life, and we can give of ourselves – that is often what it means to live forgivingly. Life is a gift. When we appreciate it, we forgive and our days are precious.

Does time heal *all* things?

Time often does heal. Certainly, it carries us through difficult times. It is then our choice to forgive, or not, and if we do we can move onwards, speeding the healing process. I should stress again that forgiveness doesn't necessarily mean forgiving the perpetrator of our hurt, but in some way living forgivingly – for instance, forgiving life for sometimes being so hard.

I've often been struck, though, by the power of time to bring about spontaneous forgiveness.

Case study: How time resolved Gareth and Barry's feud

Many years ago Gareth, who was a colleague of mine at the time, had had a dispute with a friend of his, Barry, which had developed into a full-on feud. 'For goodness sake,' I exclaimed one day, 'it's time you two forgave each other.'

'I hate him and I will *never* forgive him,' Gareth said vehemently – and meant it.

Earlier this year we met and enjoyed catching up. He mentioned that he'd gone with Barry, who I'd assumed was still his nemesis, to a social event. 'You're friends again?' I said. 'That's fantastic. But you said you'd never forgive him!'

'Did I?' he said. 'I'd forgotten. I can't even remember what it was about. It was years ago.'

So time had brought about spontaneous forgiveness between Gareth and Barry to the extent that they'd even forgotten what had passed so acrimoniously between them. I've learned since that this is what often happens. Wait long enough and time, if you don't scupper it with ongoing active resentment, often does bring about forgiveness. It may come through complete forgetfulness, as in Gareth and Barry's friendship, or because the emotions felt so acutely in the past have faded into insignificance.

Try it now: Get on with it!

But we don't have to wait to forgive. In the moment – now – you can ask yourself: 'Do I want to forgive?' Sometimes you might only realize that you do when you ask that question. Unasked, you might not know and wait unnecessarily for time to bring forgiveness and the healing it speeds. Once you give the answer 'Yes, I do', you can get on, now, with the business of forgiving.

Remember: it can cover all sorts of forgiveness – from tolerance through acceptance, understanding and compassion. Forgiveness is there waiting for you to call on it and, when you do, it will come.

Do we need to forget to forgive?

No – forgiveness is not dependent on forgetting. We choose to forgive in some way, and keep forgiving, even though we remember what happened, but we can't forget as an act of will. Sometimes time brings about a natural forgetting of a past hurt, as we saw above. We can also choose not to dwell on a memory and this is a very helpful part of the forgiving spectrum.

What we usually mean when we say we've forgotten a hurt is that we are going to dismiss any recurring thoughts or memories of it.

Yet some people assume that they need to forget to forgive and berate themselves for not being able to. 'I've tried, but I can't forget what happened' and 'I'd love to forgive her, but how can I when I can't forget?' are cries for help that I hear frequently. The relief people feel on learning that they aren't somehow inept at some special skill of forgetting or incapable of forgiving is often profound. And once they realize that they don't *have* to forget before they can forgive, forgiving becomes a real option and, often, much easier than they thought it could be.

Harnessing the natural urge to move on

Sometimes when we're very hurt or shocked, we'll find ourselves caught in a mass of negative emotions and unable to move on from them. We need to experience them, however, and in loss and bereavement grieving is an essential and therapeutic part of healing. But time is kind and wants you to move on with it. Your mind will be wanting you to do so as well – our whole physiology, indeed, is geared to healing us and restoring our balance in mind, body and soul.

It can be hard to know when the wish to tread water in our hurt and grief is good for us or when it has gone on for too long and is keeping us down, unable to start actively healing and getting on with our lives. When we're not sure if we're grieving naturally or have become chronically depressed, I've found, both personally and with clients, that it helps to be aware of the physical sensations that come to mind.

These are some of the impressions I've heard:

- ▶ 'I feel as though I'm swimming round and round in a muddy pool I can't get out of.'

- ▶ 'It's like having my feet stuck in thick treacle and I can't walk forward.'

- ▶ 'Everything's grey and dark – I feel as though I want to put the lights on in the room but they already are on.'

Descriptions like these of how we're feeling indicate that, although we want or need to move on, we have somehow got stuck in negativity and need help. When this happens forgiveness tends to get stuck, too, and can even seem impossible, so resentment and blame tend to run riot, deepening the depression. Counselling can be brilliant at helping us through such times. Studies have shown that, with well-qualified and experienced professionals, talking therapies can be very helpful. I suggest that you ask your doctor for a recommendation and referral, but you could also do some research on the Internet to see who is practising in your area with experience and qualifications particularly relevant to your situation. Talk to anyone you're considering consulting on the phone first. You need to feel comfortable with them and to sense that they are warm, encouraging, interested in your problem and supportive.

In any counselling, we need to be prepared to open up and talk – to work with the counsellor so that she or he can gain understanding and help us in the best way possible. In a way, it can be a part of the forgiving process, because, as you talk, you're beginning to express your feelings, gain an understanding of them and generally be very compassionate to yourself.

It is, of course, possible to help yourself – reading this book shows you are already prepared to do so. Be gentle but at the same time firm with yourself, and step by step you will move forwards – out of the mud, out of the darkness and back into the light of freedom where you can once again live forgivingly and mindfully.

Focus points

* You could forgive in the blink of an eye or it might take time. Having a willingness to live forgivingly is healing in itself.
* Live in the moment and live forgivingly and time will ensure ongoing healing and wellbeing.
* Be mindful – pay attention to what's going on and, above all, to your and others' feelings.
* Embrace change – it's bound to happen and it can be good.
* Remember that the past is the past. Live compassionately now and the future will look after itself.

Next step

In Chapter 20, Justice and forgiveness, we look at the way justice helps us forgive and move on.

Justice and forgiveness

In this chapter you will learn:

▶ *How forgiveness can be placed at the heart of our justice system, not to condone crime but to move beyond it*

▶ *How restorative justice can lead offenders away from a life of crime*

▶ *How restorative justice can help victims overcome the bitterness and anger they feel against those who have harmed them*

▶ *How mutual understanding, respect, fair play and clemency are key values in a forgiving society and justice system.*

Our attitude to crime and our aptitude for forgiveness tend to be a bit mixed up. For instance, we may rather admire charismatic criminals who display chutzpah and easily forgive what we see as their antics rather than evildoing. But woe betide any charmless criminals – we bay for their punishment. The same goes for those icons of perfection we've idolized – if celebrities fall from their pedestals, their admirers see it as a betrayal and turn against them in a decidedly unforgiving way.

In our own circle, we may spot a scam, fiddle or other criminal racket going on, but be reluctant to blow the whistle. We're quick to condemn the newsworthy politician and businessperson who goes off the rails, but we make light of or deny our own dishonesties.

There are, of course, degrees in everything, and each of us has to work out what we think is just and unjust, and where we stand when considering any dishonesty or wrongdoing. Justice and remedies for criminality also need a lot of thought. Any of us may become a victim of crime and we are all part of our system of justice. On the whole, this works well and we should treasure it.

Moving towards a restorative justice system

The traditional style of retributive justice aims to bring the culprit to reckoning and sentence them to a punishment that's proportionate to the crime. It's a system used throughout the world in most cultures and dates back centuries. Such punishment has normally been viewed as deserved, ethical and moral. But as our bursting-at-the-seams prisons show, it is hardly very effective either as a deterrent against new crimes or at rehabilitating convicted criminals, who all too often come out of prison only to reoffend.

So a better way is clearly much needed and today, thankfully, we are making great strides in the development of restorative justice. This is much more in line with a forgiving way of life. Thought is paid to the needs and future wellbeing of the perpetrators of crime as well as to the victims. Perpetrators are encouraged to consider the effects of their actions – not just the physical effect on their victims but the emotional repercussions as well. Empathy is something that can be learned, even by someone who has lacked an upbringing conducive to developing it. Victims take an active role, perhaps meeting or writing to the perpetrator who has harmed them in some way. In learning to take responsibility for their actions and see the full extent of the harm done, criminals:

- find that their sense of self-control and self-esteem increases

- realize that they have choices, every step of the way

- understand that they are part of a community to which and in which they and each of us have a duty to care for it and for one another

- realize that they can take a new direction in life, learning a new skill or trade, studying, and working towards a better and fulfilling way of life.

Moreover, the negativity they feel towards their victims and potential victims is transformed as they realize that they are not 'arrogant' or 'stupid' or any of the other epithets they may have thrust upon them but normal all-round people just trying to get on with their lives the best way they can.

All this has a dramatic effect on encouraging criminals to actually *want* to go straight rather than merely weighing up, as is so often the case under the retributive system, the risk of getting caught again against the benefit they can gain from a crime.

Remember this

Restorative justice helps offenders feel forgiven by society. It helps them forgive themselves. It helps them take a responsible place in society and live caringly.

As self-forgiveness is important in a forgiving society and a forgiving way of life, it's very important for offenders to make amends in some way for the harm they've caused. This could be in any of the ways we discussed in Chapter 17, Ways to help forgive and be forgiven. All the following can be life-transforming in changing the way an offender thinks about the whole concept of hurting others.

They could try:

► saying sorry to the victim

► listening to them and talking with them about what happened

► returning stolen goods

► repairing damage

► atoning when restoration is not possible, either by doing something directly for the victim, or for the victim's or their own community.

These actions can be powerfully healing for the victim, too, especially when they know that the offender will be backed up by ongoing support in leading a crime-free life.

Restorative justice like this is very people-centred. As a criminal, you are much more likely to become a responsible, law-abiding citizen if you see crime as acting against your fellow human beings – other individuals much like them – rather than against the police, magistrates and judges or the state and government, which are seen as a forbidding entity and enemy. It also tends to have a big effect in helping the victim get over what happened and forgive in some way.

As a victim, too, you are much more likely to view the criminal is a 'real' person and to realize that criminality is not innate but the result of a hotchpotch of genes, education, influences and opportunity. It takes away the culture of blame and shame and the lust for revenge. It enables compassion. It doesn't necessarily mean that you forgive them or feel you have to; neither is it in any way condoning the wrong they've done and the pain and distress they've caused. But it is part of the forgiving way – which feels so, so much better.

Believers in restorative justice are sometimes accused – as I have often been – of wearing rose-coloured spectacles. The truth, though, is plain for all to see: while retributive justice all too often leads to recidivism, restorative justice encourages offenders to become responsible, law-abiding citizens. It works well for victims of crime, too, helping them in all kinds of ways to recover from the attack or loss and enjoy life again.

Some principles of justice that are part of the forgiving way

UNDERSTANDING

The more we understand why someone has committed a crime, the easier it is to think through the situation, discuss the implications and consider the most just way to deal with the offender. When you understand not only the front-line motive for the crime but also the back story – their upbringing and emotional and social development, their state of mind at the time, their mental health – it's easier to see how they can be helped to develop a sense of responsibility and honour. Such development has a big impact on our inclination, determination and ability to steer clear of crime and live compassionately.

RESPECT

It's incredibly hard to respect someone who has hurt you and behaved abominably. But everyone I've talked to or read about who has found a way to lessen their pain and outrage in the aftermath of a crime speaks of a determination to remember that their offender is a human being who, whatever their personal opinion of them, deserves their respect. This does not mean having a good opinion of them, or condoning what they've done in any way, or forgiving them as such. It means seeing them as a fellow human being, even if we do not entirely understand what has caused them to behave as they have.

A SENSE OF FAIR PLAY

The term 'fair play' originated as a sporting term and has been particularly used in cricket. Normally in sport it means that all players abide by the rules of the game and that in any dispute the umpire decides the fair consequences of the players' actions and the way forward.

A similar kind of fair-play principle works well when we are trying to be just. Consider these meanings of fairness:

▶ It means that all concerned must strive to see what is fair and what is the right, or at least the best and fairest thing to do.

▶ It means striving for balance.

▶ It eschews the prejudice and passion that obscure the facts.

▶ It encourages a sense of proportion as well as common sense and respect for all involved.

It is a sense, above all, of morality. How can we dare to judge the 'indecency' of another if we do not strive to behave decently ourselves?

REFUSAL OR RELUCTANCE TO BLAME AND SHAME

The minute you blame someone in a hostile way – whether it's for a serious crime or a trivial offence of some kind – we enter a circle of negativity. If innocent, they will feel offended and blame you for falsely accusing them. If guilty, they are likely to nevertheless react defensively and heartily dislike you for the aggressive way you've accused them.

Remember this

The spectrum of forgiveness means approaching the person you are blaming for something with respect, level-headedness and, if you can possibly find it in yourself, compassion for their predicament.

MEDIATION

In any conflict, it can be difficult to communicate on a one-to-one basis. The help of a wise mediator can help facilitate contact and dialogue between victim and offender. A good mediator is a trouble-shooter and a peacemaker. They will not push either of you to go further or faster than you wish or feel able to; they will simply help you enter a neutral zone where understanding and respect pave the way for the victim to let go of or diminish their thoughts of ill-will and revenge, and for the offender to realize the effect of their actions and begin to take responsibility for them and think how they might make some kind of reparation for them.

CLEMENCY

This wonderful word is so apt for today in so many ways but it has fallen out of fashion. Let's use it and live it! It's about being merciful and willing to call for or accept a less severe sentence. Again, such leniency does not in any way condone the crime or show weakness. It is often brave, always compassionate and can make both the victim and the perpetrator feel better. It is very much part of the spectrum of forgiveness.

Focus points

* We're fortunate to have a justice system that works well. Let's uphold and improve it by maintaining/increasing our personal standards of behaving well, with understanding and fairness.
* Restorative justice works best – it's about understanding, forgiving, supporting and generally working to help others be responsible and caring.
* Understanding, respect for others and a sense of fair play are all part of the forgiving spectrum.
* Clemency isn't weak – it's strong and brave and helpful.

Next step

In Chapter 21, World forgiveness, we look at how a sense of fairness and a readiness to forgive among all people and nations can help us on our journey to world peace and mutual support.

World forgiveness

In this chapter you will learn:

▶ *How forgiveness can help bring about peace between peoples and nations*

▶ *How you can contribute to a global evolution towards peace, harmony and forgiveness.*

Forgiveness is a potent source of healing between nations, right around the world.

We only have to look at countries torn apart by war, genocide, rape and torture to see how millions of people can and do forgive with extraordinary generosity and compassion.

As an example, I remember as a girl being fascinated by the way my parents' generation forgave, in so many ways and degrees, the people they had fought so bitterly during the Second World War. In the wake of that devastating war, our countries became trading partners again. We helped them restore their cities and their homes. Within an incredibly short time, to my young mind, my uncle and aunt were holidaying among the very peoples who had been trying so ferociously to destroy them. Later I took part in an exchange visit with a girl whose father might well have tried to shoot down my father's plane or bomb the hospital where my mother was nursing injured troops.

There was a massive, understated but nonetheless hugely powerful wave of forgiveness. Not a forgetting, not a rose-tinted complete forgiveness of the evil initiated by the Nazi leaders, but a wish to move on from war to peace as individuals as well as nations in a mutual spirit of goodwill.

Today we are in a tide of forgiveness between nations, coming together in the present and stretching forwards to a goal of world peace. There is a sudden and growing energy as we come to realize that it isn't just a sensible idea to work together but an absolute, strident need because of climate change, population growth and fuel and food shortages. But it isn't just this need – it's a steady surging of a will to get on with others and make our world a better place to live for all. We don't want to see children dying of starvation, people tearing each other apart with cruel weapons, drugs barons destroying the happiness and health of millions. We want everyone to eat well and enjoy the abundance of the world safely, respectfully and sustainably. We want to sleep at night knowing we are doing our part in the push towards world peace.

We know it makes sense. We know it feels good. We know it is good. In fact, we know it's the only way.

Yes, it's depressing that it's not happening as fast as we would like – and sometimes it's tempting to give up and assume that the bullies and the power-hungry are winning. They are not. The countless billions of us around the world who want world peace and goodwill between all are in an overwhelming majority. We are individually and collectively realizing, more and more, that the road once less travelled is becoming our preferred and chosen one – the way of forgiveness – and we walk together holding high the standards of compassion, peace and love.

Try it now: Make a statement for world peace

Making your own statement of a world peace initiative is positive and inspiring and will – if you send it to politicians – add to the momentum for peace. You may like to use the following:

* We want justice for all.
* We want to live forgivingly.
* We want democracy.
* We want peace at home and between nations.
* We want tolerance between faiths, races and genders.
* We want a good standard of living for everyone.
* We want other living creatures and our environment to be looked after well and respected.

Our politicians and other leaders usually start out with these as their beliefs and goals, but can become jaded if they are too often thwarted and discouraged. We need to encourage them with the ongoing affirmation that the wish for goodness to prevail isn't foolish but worth upholding with all their hearts and intelligence and strength and that we are behind them.

We need to encourage each other, too, in the path of goodness and remind ourselves that the barrage of violence found across our media, from computer games to TV shows, has nothing to do with real life, and we don't want it to be. Let's keep it in perspective for what it is. Forgiving, but firmly refusing to emulate it in any way in our real lives.

Try it now: Be optimistic

When faced with others' pessimism, it helps to remember the following. The human race is very good at:

* living in the moment, not the past
* moving on from conflict
* restoring and rebuilding
* searching for better ways of living and being
* searching for ways to promote freedom and democracy
* communicating, educating and learning.

All these are part of the forgiving way of being, and as well as helping us individually they help us collectively develop a humane civilization.

Key idea

We can achieve world peace. We are already working towards it. It is possible and a forgiving way of life is at the heart of it. There are many excellent organizations working towards peace and they need our support. But it's important to remember that we can promote the forgiving way in our individual lives – at home, at work and out and about as we follow our interests. Let's remember to be thoughtful, tolerant and kind, knowing that our homes can become havens of love and happiness and our workplace a good space to be in, too.

Focus points

* Let us remember – and it's worth repeating to ourselves every day of our lives – that forgiving is about giving and that when we are compassionate, kind, generous, loving, thoughtful, honest, sensitive or fair – to others and ourselves – we are living in a forgiving way.
* Let the way of forgiveness be the way of your home environment and the whole world beyond. Take your place in it gladly.

I wish you the peace, love, happiness and joy of a forgiving way of life.

Resources

Websites

www.foundation4peace.org

www.peacefoundation.org.uk

www.theforgivenessproject.com

Books

John Bradshaw, *Creating Love* (Bantam, 1992)

Leo F. Buscaglia, *Love* (Fawcett Books, 1978)

Shakti Gawain, *Living in the Light: A Guide to Personal & Planetary Evolution*, new edition (New World Books, 1998)

Louise Hay, *You Can Heal Your Life,* new edition (Hay House UK, 1984)

Marian Partington, *If You Sit Very Still* (Vala Publishing Cooperative, 2012)

Index